Verses From Hampshire
Edited by Vivien Linton

First published in Great Britain in 2008 by:
Young Writers
Remus House
Coltsfoot Drive
Peterborough
PE2 9JX
Telephone: 01733 890066
Website: www.youngwriters.co.uk

All Rights Reserved

© Copyright Contributors 2008

SB ISBN 978-1 84431 664 9

Foreword

Young Writers was established in 1991 and has been passionately devoted to the promotion of reading and writing in children and young adults ever since. The quest continues today. Young Writers remains as committed to the nurturing of poetic and literary talent as ever.

This year's Young Writers competition has proven as vibrant and dynamic as ever and we are delighted to present a showcase of the best poetry from across the UK and in some cases overseas. Each poem has been selected from a wealth of *Little Laureates 2008* entries before ultimately being published in this, our seventeenth primary school poetry series.

Once again, we have been supremely impressed by the overall quality of the entries we have received. The imagination, energy and creativity which has gone into each young writer's entry made choosing the poems a challenging and often difficult but ultimately hugely rewarding task - the general high standard of the work submitted ensured this opportunity to bring their poetry to a larger appreciative audience.

We sincerely hope you are pleased with this final collection and that you will enjoy *Little Laureates 2008 Verses From Hampshire* for many years to come.

Contents

Church Crookham Junior School

Jordan Cox (9)	1
Natascha Oakes (8)	1
Michael Duemke (7)	2
Katie Laing (8)	2
Katie Brownbridge (7)	2
Tiegan Baxter (7)	3
Hannah Foster (8)	3
George Coster (8)	3
Emily Oldham (9)	4
Jack Killick (9)	4
Daniel Finnerty (9)	4
Bethinn Allison (9)	5
Sophia Bainbridge (7)	5
Charlie Fright (9)	5
Cameron Hughes (8)	6
Lucy Hare (9)	6
Erin Blackburn (10)	6
Katie Mullin (10)	7
Kate Williams (9)	7
Connor Findley (10)	7
Karis Winning (10)	8
Josh Westwood (9)	8
Alex Harvey (8)	9
Jake Milstead (9)	9
Emily Aston (9)	10
Francesca Newman (9)	10
Nathan Warwick (9)	10
James Dudley (7)	11
Callum Mackenzie (7)	11
Charlotte Fox (8)	11
Jamie Camozzi (8)	12
Jasmine Newby (9)	12
Chloe Nettleton (8)	12
William Stevens (9)	13
Toby Thorne (8)	13
Jodie Hallmark (7)	13
Jack Williams (9)	14
Tiana Walden (7)	14

Amy Roberts (8)	14
Jamie Williams (8)	15
Emily Bringloe (8)	15
Joshua Kenton (7)	15
Billy Nickless (9)	16
Joshua Ingate (8)	16
Brad Hawkett (7)	16
Sophie Lowe (11)	17
Michael Hannam (11)	17
Benedict Roose (8)	18
Amber De-Terville (8)	18
Lewis Shadrake (8)	18
Leah Garvey (7)	19
Chris Malyon (8)	19
Amy White (8)	19
Eloise Lewis (7)	20
Megan Aston (8)	20
Caitlin Pirie (7)	20
Tess Ebner (7)	21
Kai Walker (7)	21
Lucy James (8)	21
Alice Beegan (7)	22
Charlie Machon (7)	22
Mollie Bennett	22
James Smith (10)	23
Connor Ricketts (7)	23
Mica-Anne Harris (7)	23
Anna Wright (10)	24
Tyreese Lewis (7)	24
Aaron Pennell (7)	24
Hope Clarke (11)	25
Brogen De Roeck (7)	25
Madeleine Hughes (11)	26
Edward Scott-South (8)	26
Jessica Benson (7)	26
James Wyatt (10)	27
Tudor McManus (9)	27
Grace Unwin (8)	27
Samantha Dunn (10)	28
Kirsty Bradley (9)	28
Megan Reece (11)	29
Amber Lloyd (8)	29

Matthew Knock (10)	30
Joe Elliott (9)	30
Emily Harris (9)	30
Robert Earls (10)	31
Lewis Charlie Moore (9)	31
Imogen Frances Read (9)	31
Ryan Williams (9)	32
Cameo Louise Lang (11)	32
Savannah Buckle (10)	32
Georgia Sheepwash (9)	33
Michael Colfer (8)	33
Chloe Eloise Jackson (10)	34
Jamie Bailey (9)	34
Alexander Higgins (10)	35
Ella Boulton (7)	35
Katie Rose Deans (9)	35
Thomas Edwards (9)	36
Callum Mercer (9)	36
Phoebe Robinson (9)	37
Gemma Burge (9)	37
Annie Rose James (8)	37
George Davis (8)	38
Olivia McKeon (9)	38
Cameron Higgins (8)	38
Michaela Child (10)	39
Daniel Pesquero (9)	39
Matthew Swan (8)	39
Chloe Davies (10)	40
Jake Francis (10)	40
Jonathan Hillson (11)	41
Declan Downey (8)	41
Olivia Rideout (10)	42
Chloe McDonald (8)	42
Sian Hundley (8)	42
Kieran Sheepwash (11)	43
Jamie Mullin (8)	43
Sophie Cairns (7)	43
Zoe Westwood (11)	44
Grace Mayhew (10)	44
Oliver Bainbridge (10)	45
Thomas Potter (7)	45
James King (9)	45

Grace Young (10)	46
Sam Killick (7)	46
Adam Crumpton (7)	46
Adam Bolton (7)	47
Dominic Leigh Horton (9)	47
Caitlin Davis (10)	47
Mark Walter (7)	48
Oliver Sanderson (7)	48
Caitlin Stewart (7)	48
William Lloyd (7)	49
Matthew Fordham (8)	49
Matthew Tyler (10)	49
Sophie Ellis (10)	50
Peter Bolton (10)	50
Alastair Lee (10)	50
Jamie House (7)	51
Becky Wall (9)	51
Bethany Middleton (8)	51
Madi Bate (7)	52
Megan Price (8)	52
Jasmine Price (8)	52
Gemma Morgan (8)	53
Emily McCulloch (8)	53
Bethan Davies (7)	53
Thomas Vickery (7)	54
Douglas Critchley (8)	54
Lili Swain (8)	54
Joe Hutton (10)	55
Charlie Crumpton (9)	55
Holly Geall (9)	55
Tiegan Skinner (9)	56
Daniel Gray (10)	56
Daniel Campbell (10)	56
Alexandra Laing (9)	57
Helen Walter (9)	57
Travis Milton (9)	57
Semiti Marautaki (9)	58
Ellis Hardy (9)	58
Thomas Davies (9)	58
Vicki Lee Duemke (9)	59
Robert Colfer (10)	59
Hannah Neil (9)	59

Megan Benson (9)	60
Courtney Louise Chilvers (8)	60
Marina Fedoroff (9)	60
Chelsie Gray (9)	61
Lauren Vickery (8)	61
James Burrell (8)	61
Hannah Phillipou (9)	62
Joshua Atkinson (9)	62
Eleanor Hobby (8)	62
Connie Margaret Rolls (9)	63
Katie Wakelin (9)	63
Nathan Charles Kingham (9)	63
Bethany Louise Gray (8)	64
Shaun Kern (8)	64
John Roome (9)	64
Siân Roberts (10)	65
Keeley Ducker (11)	65
Jack Garvey (10)	66
Rebecca Consterdine (10)	66
Jack Chapman (10)	67

Oakridge Junior School

Ugnius Zelba (11)	67
Isobel Tennison (11)	68
Joseph Clarke (9)	68
Connor O'Brien (10)	68
Zack Gill (7)	69
Paul Izzard (8)	69
Cade Martin (8)	69
Maisy McDonough-Dancer (10)	70
Kelsey Mosquera (9)	70
Jessica Bridgeman (10)	70
Lauren Paine (10)	71
Jessica Muller (10)	71
Kyra Wright (11)	71
Chloe Brede (9)	72
Sallyann Blanchard (11)	72
Jasmin Lee (10)	72
Melissa Gallop (9)	72
Carah Newlands (11)	73
Lauren-Rose Lambert (9)	73

Rhys Dawkins (10)	73
George McRae (10)	74
Shane Paterson (11)	74
Eleanor Jeffery (9)	74
Luka Virgilio (9)	75
Rachel Bennett (10)	75
Adam Richardson (10)	75
Oliver Lucas (9)	76
Patrick Fastnedge (8)	76
Megan Orton (9)	76
Lucy Smith (8)	77
Georgia Bicknell (9)	77
Holly McCann (8)	77
Cally Pettifor (9)	78
Dylan Jones (8)	78
Kaaviya Rajapakeerathan (9)	78
Georgia Harwood (8)	79
Belle Wrangles (7)	79
Chloe Flores (9)	79
Oris Shenyan (10)	80
Joshua Andrews (8)	80
James Beeden (10)	80
Tommy Barkham (8)	81
Nick Frazer (10)	81
Lorelei Nielsen (9)	81
Joshua Blaber (10)	82
Philly Holden (10)	82
Riley Fenn (9)	82
Mary Roberts (11)	83
Alex Downham (9)	83
Georgia Ariss (11)	83
Craig Niven (11)	83
Courtney Clement (10)	84
Nicole Coyle (10)	84
Lisa Bartlett (11)	84
Joseph Smith (10)	85
Sheyanne Tedford (9)	85
Tegan Ledger (9)	85
Cathan Eames (9)	86

Portway Junior School

Hannah Allmark & Cerys Cousins (9)	86
Lauryn Newman (8)	87
Siân Allen (9) & Tayla Jade Moody (8)	87
Courtney Tobin (9)	88
Abigail Jones (9)	88
Kayleigh Morris (8)	89
Cara-Leigh Bishop & Gemma Bennett (9)	89
Mikela Donnelly (9)	90
Charlene Dible (9)	90
Chloe Brookes (8) & Lizzie White (9)	91
Dana Shelley (9)	92
Liam Russell (9)	92
Jing-Ying Wong (9)	93
Ronan White (9)	93
Alex Morling (9)	94
Harvey Sullivan (9)	94
Matthew Corbett (8)	95
Cassie Clementine Shearer (8)	95
Stanley North (8)	96
Hannah Sullivan (8)	96
Hannah Wood (9)	97
Hayden Coyne (8)	97
Jordan Day (9)	98
Amber Casselton (9)	98
Moath Alshryfat (9)	99
Luke Holden (8)	99
Charlie Rogers (8)	100
Kerry Louise Allen & Jessica-Leigh Nixon (9)	100
Declan Hughes (9)	101
Alex Roberts (9) & Jenny Upton (8)	101
Gregor Corcoran (8)	102

Stoke Park Junior School

Abby Arnold (11)	102
Aleesha Head (10)	103
Lewis Dawkins (10)	103
Jed Ponsford (10)	104
Charley Snow (11)	104
Gemma Bevis-Lacey (10)	105
Ben Haynes (10)	105

Ashlee Moore	106
Sophie Townsend (8)	106
Abbie Carter (11)	107
Christopher Hopkins (10)	107
Isobel Hardy (10)	108
Isaac Porter (8)	108
Bethany Vokes (8)	109
Kierney Frampton (7)	109
Daniel Brierley (8)	110
Elena Beckett-Oxenham (7)	110
Kyle Patel (8)	111
Georgia Hall (10)	111
Lauren Foster (10)	112
Rachel Thompson (11)	113
Olivia Norman (7)	113
Ben Bramall, Joshua Hughes, Simon Hancock, Harley White, Adam Wastney (7), Ciarán Cooper & Aidan Asquith (8)	114
Daniel Hibberd (9)	114
Keiran Murray (9)	115
Georgia Blake (9)	115
Chloe Jarvis (10)	116
Abi Carr (9)	117
Jack Horn (10)	118
Gregory Lay (10)	118
Natasha Keith (9)	119
Lauren Powell (10)	119
Bradley Reeves (10)	120
James Ross (10)	121
James Dilworth (10)	122
Ashleigh Curl (10)	122
Harriet Johnson (10)	123
Andrew Pritchard (11)	123
Bailey Moore (9)	124
Fraser McGowan (10)	124
Summer Hammond (10)	125
Max Copsey (9)	125
Holly Mumford (10)	126
Luke Baker (9)	126
Jenna Anderson (9)	127
Charlie Andrews (10)	127
Jim Dawkins (9)	128
Jack Bailey (11)	128

James Wheable (10)	129
Summah Walker (10)	129
Andrew Wood (10)	130
Tammy Dunford (11)	130
Heather Thomson (10)	131
Anne Pritchard (9)	132
Leila Harding (10)	132
Ellen Cosgrove (10)	133
Harry Salmon (9)	134
Dan Page (11)	135
Martha Richmond (10)	136
Daniel Lipscombe (10)	137
James Thomas (11)	137
Mollie Young (10)	138
Timothy Arthur (10)	139
James Hunt (11)	140
Alice Warne (10)	141
Ian Bevan (10)	142
Daniel Kane (10)	143
Lauren Atkins (10)	144
Sergio Mucci (10)	145
Courtney Richmond (11)	146
Jack Howson (10)	147
Amelia Humphries (11)	148
Callum Holmes (10)	149
Joe Perrett (10)	150

Wellow Primary School

James Brand (9)	151
Ross Weeks (10)	152
Dev Daas (9)	153
Cara Young (9)	154
Laura Overton-Hore (10)	155
Kyran Hansford (11)	156
Annabel Skinner (9)	157
Kyle Russell Blakey (11)	158
Harry Chapman (10)	159
Lauren Williams (10)	160
Rhiannon Lloyd Leighton (9)	161
Grace Oreffo (10)	162
Adam Cater (10)	163

Monica Young (9)	164
Edward Barnes (10)	165
Dan Cullen (9)	166
Eleanor Sandison (10)	167
Oliver Lambert (9)	168
Jackson Howell (9)	169
Simon Lockyer (10)	170
Daniel Williams (10)	171

The Poems

Emotions

Happiness is . . .
A dreamful day under the sun,
Someone giving you the perfect gift,
A baby girl like the messy new queen!
People giving you your favourite chocolates,
A hot, beautiful holiday with your family.

Sadness is . . .
You getting told off by your mother
Who is trying her very best to keep you under control.
You getting vegetables for a whole week.
A member of your family moving a long, long way away.

Anger is . . . you getting so annoyed at yourself and
You get seven years of bad luck
Because you smashed a mirror.
A thing that you always dreamt of is now gone
And will never meet your fast-beating heart.
You get angry at your friends and
You never get back together because of your . . . *anger.*

Jordan Cox (9)
Church Crookham Junior School

Animal Safety

When you happily have a beautiful day
You can see the creatures like
A bird in the tree with her babies
And she feeds them.
As well you can sea the creatures in the sea
Like starfish and you can see
The great white shark.
When you see creatures on the road,
Like a zebra crossing, you have to stop
And do not run over them.

Natascha Oakes (8)
Church Crookham Junior School

Mystery

Mystery is black like a vampire's fingerprint on the door.
It sounds like a ghost haunting this house now.
It smells like a ghost's breath in the dark, dark night.
It looks like some smoke coming through the door.
It feels like ghosts breathing on me.
It reminds me of my Scooby Doo game.

Michael Duemke (7)
Church Crookham Junior School

Mystery

Mystery is black like the night sky with no light.
It sounds like the rustling of trees slowly moving.
It smells like smelly fish slithering through the sea.
It looks like an evil person dressed up as a monster.
It feels like a crinkled piece of bacon in the cooker.
It reminds me of a werewolf howling at the night sky.

Katie Laing (8)
Church Crookham Junior School

Adventure

Adventure is blue like a big, handsome whale.
It sounds like the deep, wide sea washing through my ears.
It smells like the smell of smelly saltwater.
It looks like a bath overflowing.
It feels like a shark under my feet.
It reminds me of a puffer fish putting spikes in my feet.

Katie Brownbridge (7)
Church Crookham Junior School

Adventure

Adventure is crystal blue like the salty sea.
It sounds like a pot of salt rustling in my ear.
It smells like a seaside picnic just for you and me.
It looks like the waves of the salty blue sea crashing against me.
It feels like the boat is going to crash into some sharp rocks.
It reminds me of my big diving adventure!

Tiegan Baxter (7)
Church Crookham Junior School

Mystery

Mystery is red like a burning sun.
It sounds like little mice squeaking up the path.
It smells like disgusting red blood.
It looks like teacher being disgusting.
It feels like sloppy sick.
It reminds me of going to the zoo.

Hannah Foster (8)
Church Crookham Junior School

Mystery

Mystery is white like you are so scared.
It sounds like giant ghosts moaning loudly.
It smells like fire burning in the sky.
It looks like a giant spider on my wall.
It feels like I am growing hairs.
It reminds me of Scooby Doo!

George Coster (8)
Church Crookham Junior School

Frustration

Frustration is a blur of colours mixing together.
It sounds like someone screaming beside me.
It's a piece of cod burning on the boiling stove.
Frustration tastes like smoke coming from your nose into your mouth.
It reminds me of cooking which is going wrong.
It feels like dying.
Frustration is like being stuck in a huge maze, all alone.

Emily Oldham (9)
Church Crookham Junior School

Laughter

Laughter is a jumping joke floating through your head.
Laughter is pale blue like the sky above.
Laughter is a ball of fun in the air.
It is always lovely when you say laughter.
People love laughter, laughter, laughter.

Jack Killick (9)
Church Crookham Junior School

Anger

Anger is red like an exploding volcano.
It's a sword being pulled from its case.
It tastes like a sour lemon running down my throat.
It smells like smoke flying from fire.

Daniel Finnerty (9)
Church Crookham Junior School

Love

Love is a dove soaring above.
Love is pink like a heart.
Love smells like roses from the start.
Love sounds like birds singing in the sky.
Love reminds me of clouds up so high.
Love tastes like chocolate.
Love is happiness.

Bethinn Allison (9)
Church Crookham Junior School

Mystery

Mystery is blue like the deep blue sea.
It sounds like a ghost creeping up behind me.
It smells like vampires flying in the night sky.
It looks like a ghost flying around my house.
It feels like a jelly slithering through my hands.
It reminds me of my hair standing on end!

Sophia Bainbridge (7)
Church Crookham Junior School

Darkness

Darkness is grey and black like midnight sky.
Darkness is people crying.
Darkness smells like fresh blood.
Darkness reminds me that people die.
Darkness tastes like red blood.

Charlie Fright (9)
Church Crookham Junior School

Adventure

Adventure is blue like the big, deep ocean.
It sounds like a whale chasing after me.
It smells like the rotten seaweed tangled round my feet.
It looks like a shark speaking to me.
It feels like I'm touching a killer whale.
It reminds me of swimming in the ocean.

Cameron Hughes (8)
Church Crookham Junior School

Fear

Fear is when the light goes out!
The taste is of animals' blood.
A monster under your bed.
Fear is when your hair sticks up on end.
It is the colour of red and black, just like a vampire.
Fear is watching you when you go to bed!

Lucy Hare (9)
Church Crookham Junior School

Anger

Anger is red like fierce fire,
It is like thunder crashing all the time through the night.
It tastes like hot chillies burning down your throat.
Anger reminds you of the darkness all around.
It smells of the smoke coming from the red fire.
Anger is death.

Erin Blackburn (10)
Church Crookham Junior School

Sadness

Sadness is blue like a sparkling turquoise sea of tears.
It sounds like slow, steady waves
Lapping onto a silent sandy beach.
It tastes like a cold glass of tasteless water.
It smells like a cold, musty mist filling my nose.
It looks like an empty grey room that imprisons you.
It feels like a cold, damp day with fog
Enclosing you from the rest of the world.

Katie Mullin (10)
Church Crookham Junior School

Fun

Fun tastes like the sweetest lollipop.
It reminds me of the good times, laughing and chatting.
Fun smells like sugar and sweetness combining with each other.
The joy feels like a blossom tree sprouting.
Fun is multicoloured just like a rainbow emerging from the sky.
My nose smells it like a drip of sparkling water, so tender and mild.

Kate Williams (9)
Church Crookham Junior School

Hate

Hate is devils and angels face to face.
Hate is black like the midnight sky.
It sounds like bombs exploding in a battlefield.
It tastes like fresh blood.
Hate smells like a burning thunder ball.

Connor Findley (10)
Church Crookham Junior School

Imagine Being Lonely

How would you feel if you were
The only person left in the world?
        . . . lonely . . .
                . . . lonely . . .
                        . . . lonely . . .
If you called 999 and no one picked up!
                      . . . lonely . . .
            . . . lonely . . .
    . . . lonely . . .
Imagine having no friends, family or pets.
Scared or hurt, sad or jealous,
There is no one there to help.

You're on your own,
The lights go out . . .

Karis Winning (10)
Church Crookham Junior School

Anger

Anger is fiery red like a flowing river of
Molten lava burning through everything.
It sounds like a newborn screeching in its hunger.
It tastes like a hot, spicy chilli pepper
Burning inside your mouth.
It smells like a hot, stuffy room
Overflowing with steam.
It looks like a charging T-rex
Going down for its prey.
It feels like fire melting through your hands.
It reminds me of revenge on
All the things I've done wrong.

Josh Westwood (9)
Church Crookham Junior School

Emotions

Anger is black as a moonless night.
Anger is a hot flame.
Anger is a tiger looking for food.
Anger is the second world war.

Happiness is pink like a mermaid's tail.
Happiness is the sun.
Happiness is a bunny bouncing in grass.
Happiness is a fairground.

Fun is yellow like the sun.
Fun is a holiday.
Fun is a cute kitten.
Fun is a trampoline.

Alex Harvey (8)
Church Crookham Junior School

I'm Rich!

I'm rich! I have a mansion.
I'm rich! I have a train.
I'm rich! I don't have rations.
I'm rich! I don't get pains.

I'm rich! I have an aeroplane.
I'm rich! I am the boss.
I'm rich! I just gain everything.
I'm rich! I have a loss.

My loss is
My daddy's dead.
Boohoo!

Jake Milstead (9)
Church Crookham Junior School

Happiness

Happiness is yellow like the glistening sun.
Happiness sounds like a flutter of laughter.
Happiness tastes like a sweet toffee melting on my tongue.
Happiness smells like a lily slipping up my nose.
Happiness looks like a field of flowers chuckling away.
Happiness feels like a clown making me grin.
Happiness reminds me of a playground of children giggling at me.

Emily Aston (9)
Church Crookham Junior School

Happiness

Happiness is golden like the sun shining on a hot sunny day.
It sounds like a pod of dolphins singing a happy song.
It tastes like a spicy curry being served on a table.
It smells like a daffodil floating its perfumed smell around.
It feels like a grain of gold hovering in the air.
It reminds me of a butterfly taking pollen from a flower.

Francesca Newman (9)
Church Crookham Junior School

Anger

Anger is red like a stream of boiling-hot lava.
It sounds like a fierce erupting volcano.
It tastes like shepherd's pie running down my throat.
It smells like smoke from a cigarette burning in my mouth.
It looks like a swarm of angry bees heading for my head.
It feels like red-hot chillies burning in my mouth.

Nathan Warwick (9)
Church Crookham Junior School

Mystery

A mystery is scary like someone watching you.
It sounds like a spirit going *mmm, mmm*.
It smells of invisible mist.
It looks like a gremlin with really sharp gnashers.
It feels like a hairy spider crawling over my face.
It reminds me of when my uncle died.

James Dudley (7)
Church Crookham Junior School

Adventure

Adventure is green like a round cucumber.
It sounds like eating the green skin.
It smells like a hot bonfire.
It looks like the dark sky.
It feels like hot air.
It reminds me of bats.

Callum Mackenzie (7)
Church Crookham Junior School

Adventure

Adventure is yellow like a sizzling, hot sun.
It sounds like some creepy hands clapping.
It smells like a huge barbecue of hot burgers.
It looks like some black ghosts and purple ants.
It feels like witches are pulling me to pieces.
It reminds me of a creepy movie I watched.

Charlotte Fox (8)
Church Crookham Junior School

Adventure

Adventure is grey like metal
That people use to build roller coasters.
It sounds like screws banging on the metal
When it's being built.
It looks like a very scary ride
Down that steep drop.
It feels like my stomach
Is flying out of my empty body.
It reminds me of creepy ghosts
Stealing my soul.

Jamie Camozzi (8)
Church Crookham Junior School

I'm Staying At Home From School Today

I'm staying at home from school today,
I really must admit,
All the LSAs laugh at me
And every time I cry.
All the children run away
And call me Snoozy Sue,
That is why I'm not arriving at class,
All I did was snooze in school!
Hope my students don't find out.

Jasmine Newby (9)
Church Crookham Junior School

Adventure

Adventure is like a beautiful yellow shining sun.
It sounds like the birds singing and tweeting
It smells like fresh spring flowers.

Chloe Nettleton (8)
Church Crookham Junior School

Opposite Emotions

Happiness tastes like a fresh dandelion.
Happiness feels like a hot summer's day.
Happiness sounds like someone laughing.
Happiness looks like an angel.

Anger tastes like red-hot sauce.
Anger feels like you have gone to Hell.
Anger looks like a devil.
Anger is a poisonous spider.

William Stevens (9)
Church Crookham Junior School

Adventure

Adventure is like raging rocks tumbling down.
It sounds like the sea crashing in a seashell.
It looks like freezing ice cream in a yummy cone.
It feels like a bumpy road with tiny rocks.
It reminds me of sleeping in a cosy bed,
Frightened of what will happen tomorrow.

Toby Thorne (8)
Church Crookham Junior School

Adventure

Adventure is brown like a teddy bear.
It sounds like a bear growling at me.
It smells like a baby.
It looks like a baby.
It feels soft.
It reminds me of a dog.

Jodie Hallmark (7)
Church Crookham Junior School

Emotions

Anger tastes of burned sausages sizzling on your tongue.
Anger sounds like a train sounding its horn inside you.

Sadness is a cold, snowy January day.
Sadness is death.

Happiness is the whole world falling down with laughter.
Happiness is the smell of food climbing up your nose.

Jack Williams (9)
Church Crookham Junior School

Adventure

Adventure is blue like a bright sunny sky.
It sounds like birds tweeting in their warm, cuddly nests.
It smells like people cooking hard, spicy ginger.
It looks like people smiling at their best friends.
It feels like the wind blowing into your hands.
It reminds me of playing in the exciting park!

Tiana Walden (7)
Church Crookham Junior School

Mystery

Mystery is creepy like a scratching, slurping vampire.
It sounds like someone screaming in their gloomy, dark room.
It smells like a tiny, hard bullet just been shot from a rusty gun.
It looks like terror, tingling down my wobbly spine.
It feels like a cold little creature all crumpled up.
It reminds me of waking up after the scariest dream in the universe.

Amy Roberts (8)
Church Crookham Junior School

The Adventure

An adventure is green like freezing cold grass.
It sounds like tiny footsteps haunting up the path.
It smells like chickens in a smelly building.
It looks like scary ghosts running through the night.
It feels like terror running through my clenching body.
It reminds me of zooming up in the night
With my hair standing on end!

Jamie Williams (8)
Church Crookham Junior School

Adventure

Adventure is red like lips in disasters.
It sounds like lions growling at me!
It smells like lovely roses with some writing on them.
It looks like blackcurrant juice.
It feels like someone being hurt.
It reminds me of my mum when she had a bleeding eye.

Emily Bringloe (8)
Church Crookham Junior School

Adventure

Adventure is yellow like a boiling hot sun.
It sounds like lions growling at me.
It smells like coconut trees swaying in the breeze.
It looks like zombies staring at me.
It feels like horror going into me.
It reminds me of Hallowe'en.

Joshua Kenton (7)
Church Crookham Junior School

Balls Can Fly

Balls can fly,
Balls can shoot,
Balls can fire,
Balls can hurt.

Balls are round,
Balls are leather,
Balls are hard,
Balls are bouncy.

Balls can destroy,
Balls can pop,
Balls can smash,
Balls can break.

Billy Nickless (9)
Church Crookham Junior School

Adventure

Adventure is red like a hot volcano.
It sounds like a giant bang.
It smells like hot lava.
It feels like I am going to explode.
It reminds me of hot tea.

Joshua Ingate (8)
Church Crookham Junior School

Mystery

Mystery s black like black, soggy blood.
It sounds like people running down corridors.
It smells like fire.
It feels like a breeze is hitting me.

Brad Hawkett (7)
Church Crookham Junior School

Love

Love is a heart,
Floating and dreaming.
Love is a rose,
Gleaming and sparkling.
Love is a smile
That lasts forever.
Love is sweetness,
Love is beautiful.

Love is a secret passion,
Forgiving and forgetting.
Love is a battle
Between the two.
Love is an emotion
That travels through your heart.
Love is a sweet smell,
Love is bittersweet.

Sophie Lowe (11)
Church Crookham Junior School

Bruin

He was my hero,
He was my friend,
He smelt like chocolate
And felt fluffy.

My life is a puzzle
With one missing piece,
But I know that death
Will not pull us apart.

Michael Hannam (11)
Church Crookham Junior School

Adventure

Adventure is orange like a huge fire.
It sounds like a hooting, floating ghost.
It smells like the dark, dark woods.
It looks like a vampire.
It feels like terror spreading through my body.
It reminds me of waking up so scared
That I am unable to get sleep.

Benedict Roose (8)
Church Crookham Junior School

Mystery

Mystery is suspicious like a figure stalking you.
It sounds like high girly screams coming through the walls.
It smells like horror and people shrieking for help in elevators.
It looks like devils collecting evil pollen.
It feels like fear running through my veins.
It reminds me of the time I went on a spooky ghost train.

Amber De-Terville (8)
Church Crookham Junior School

Fun

Fun is yellow like a trophy.
Fun is all chasing a ball.
Fun feels like friendship.
Fun reminds me of my old friends.
Fun smells like tea at a sleepover.
Fun tastes like chocolate bars.

Lewis Shadrake (8)
Church Crookham Junior School

Adventure

Adventure is new like a new-born baby.
It sounds like big dogs thumping their small paws on the ground.
It smells like the sea making the biggest waves you have ever seen!
It looks like fish in the ocean that have just arrived.
It feels like balloons tapping me on the shoulder
Like they just want to be massive friends.
It reminds me of big hugs because adventure is
All about having fun and taking part.

Leah Garvey (7)
Church Crookham Junior School

Mystery

Mystery is red like Mars.
It sounds like a spirit howling.
It smells like a Dalek that makes you cry.
It looks like a ghost howling.
It feels like a ghost's stabbing me.
It reminds me of a robber robbing me.

Chris Malyon (8)
Church Crookham Junior School

Adventure

Adventure is green like peaceful swaying grass.
It sounds like tiny little beetles scuttling around.
It smells like strong, sweet lavender.
It looks like a colourful fountain reflecting colours from the sky.
It reminds me of my old garden.

Amy White (8)
Church Crookham Junior School

Adventure

Adventure is blue like a fast, speedy boat.
It sounds like a swishing, swashing angry sea.
It smells like rotten red apples with a loud crunchy crunch to them.
It looks like a fish swimming in the adventurous sea.
It feels like a hard, wooden plank.
It reminds me of the freezing cold breeze.

Eloise Lewis (7)
Church Crookham Junior School

Mystery

Mystery is black like the night sky.
It sounds like the wind blowing through my ears.
It smells like blood in my nose.
It looks like birds' feathers floating in the night sky.
It feels like foxes running after me.
It reminds me of running away from bears.

Megan Aston (8)
Church Crookham Junior School

Mystery

Mystery is red like hot, hot lava.
It sounds like people running for their lives.
It smells like cold, cold water.
It looks like lions trying to eat me.
It feels like tigers' teeth going through my hands.
It reminds me of vampires wanting my red blood.

Caitlin Pirie (7)
Church Crookham Junior School

Adventure

Adventure is black like your bedroom when you turn out the light.
It sounds like a rainforest where all the birds are chattering.
It smells like fresh air brushing through my nose.
It looks like a stripy tiger stalking its prey.
It feels like a furry monster's soft fur.
It reminds me of climbing the tallest tree.

Tess Ebner (7)
Church Crookham Junior School

Adventure

Adventure is exciting like someone's birthday.
It sounds like a noisy playground rushing through the wind.
It smells like a mouldy pear in someone's smelly house.
It looks like a pot of shiny gold money.
It feels like some thunder going on me.
It reminds me of a hot cup of tea.

Kai Walker (7)
Church Crookham Junior School

Adventure

Adventure is black like a night with no moon.
It sounds like a ghost giggling at me.
It smells like Coke fizzing at me.
It looks like a star shooting through the sky.
It feels like a ghost going through my body.
It reminds me of seeing a vampire!

Lucy James (8)
Church Crookham Junior School

Adventure

Adventure is blue like the deep, blue sea.
It sounds like shuffled cards getting ready to play.
It smells like smoke swooping out of a burning bonfire.
It looks like ghosts appearing from nowhere.
It feels like blood in my nose.
It reminds me of smelly fish!

Alice Beegan (7)
Church Crookham Junior School

Adventure

Adventure is black like a big, black cat.
It sounds like a big spider crawling up my back.
It smells like smoke coming out of my bedroom window.
It looks like a ghost chasing me.
It feels like a spider crawling over me.
It reminds me of everything swirling around my head.

Charlie Machon (7)
Church Crookham Junior School

Adventure

Adventure is orange like amazing sun.
It sounds like the sea shimmering on the beach.
It smells like fresh air from the wind.
It looks like a blazing fire.
It feels like a fluffy monster.
It reminds me of running down the field.

Mollie Bennett
Church Crookham Junior School

Anger

Anger is a red-hot chilli,
It's so hot I said, 'I'm so silly.'

Anger is a yellow flame,
It crackles so loud it could be in pain.

Anger is an orange spice,
It boils and bubbles and makes it taste nice.

Anger is a black shadow,
Dark and creepy but turns you mad though.

James Smith (10)
Church Crookham Junior School

Adventure

Adventure is like discovering a mystery.
It sounds like a really superb adventure.
It smells like smelly water.
It looks like an exciting adventure.
It feels like the bark on the ground is going in my shoe.
It reminds me of my birthday when I went to France.

Connor Ricketts (7)
Church Crookham Junior School

Adventure

Adventure is amazing, like super.
It smells like surprised.
It looks like exciting.
It's frightful.
It reminds me of me.

Mica-Anne Harris (7)
Church Crookham Junior School

Emotions

Happiness tastes like sweet strawberries
As red as a crimson rose.
But it can fade, turn into grey,
Turn into devastating sadness.
Then someone arrives,
They fill your heart with joy.
Love, an emotion.

Anger is a volcano burning up inside you.
It goes right to the very tip of your tongue,
Then out comes your anger,
Bang!

Anna Wright (10)
Church Crookham Junior School

Adventure

It looks like an exciting adventure
And I really want to go on it.
It feels like I am flying in the sky.
It reminds me of when I was eating some pizza.

Tyreese Lewis (7)
Church Crookham Junior School

Adventure

Adventure is green like in the wood.
It sounds like birds singing in the air.
It smells like creepy stuff around you.
It looks like creatures around you.

Aaron Pennell (7)
Church Crookham Junior School

Proud

Golden eagles showing their strength,
Shining in the sunlight,
No one can ever put them down,
They always want to be in the crowd.

Golden lions shaking their manes,
Their powerful roar echoing through the valleys,
Hiding in the long golden grass,
Lying in the bush's shade.

This is . . . proud!

Golden sun, a burning star,
Showing itself to the world,
Giving to the universe non-stop,
It never, ever stops shining.

Golden autumn leaves falling off trees,
Covering the ground like a blanket,
Being blown around by the wind,
They like to be seen everywhere during autumn.

This is . . . proud!

Hope Clarke (11)
Church Crookham Junior School

Adventure

Adventure is amazing like different animals.
It sounds like a discovery.
It looks like a frightful king.
It feels like a world of dream.
It reminds me of my holiday.

Brogen De Roeck (7)
Church Crookham Junior School

Love

Love is a flower escaping from the fresh golden soil.
Love is a beautiful smell that won't go away.
Love is deadly and can strike at any time.
Love will survive forever . . .

True love will never let you down.
Love is the only one.
Love made you and me and forever more.

Love is a feeling trapped inside.
Love is a memory that will never escape.
Love lasts a lifetime.
Love is all we have . . .

Madeleine Hughes (11)
Church Crookham Junior School

Mystery

Mystery is black like the dark, night sky.
It sounds like big, loud voices talking in the dark.
It smells like smoke from a sizzling fire.
It looks like a vampire walking in the dark.
It feels like fear rattling through my bones.
It reminds me of a ghost staring straight at me.

Edward Scott-South (8)
Church Crookham Junior School

Adventure

Adventure is white like ghosts spooking me out.
It sounds like howling and moaning at me.
It smells like fire and all smoky.
It looks like robots and mummies walk towards me.
It feels like blood running down me.
It reminds me of falling in the sea.

Jessica Benson (7)
Church Crookham Junior School

Emotions

Anger is a pile of red chillies
Burning up inside me.
As the feeling starts to grow,
It feels like I'm going to blow.

Confusion is a big brown sausage,
Sizzling and bubbling up,
Making me go *hmmm . . . ?*
But it won't be there forever because I'll catch tomorrow!

Misery is black paint,
Gets brushed over inside of me.
It causes me to be sad,
But nevertheless it goes as I cheer up quite slow.

Now sadness is another story,
A dark purple door that can lock me inside forever,
Until I break free of this curse
Then run around knowing I'm free!

James Wyatt (10)
Church Crookham Junior School

Love Is . . .

Like a big fat cuddly bear . . .
A big, beautiful birthday present . . .
As big as a building . . .
A big fat hug!

Tudor McManus (9)
Church Crookham Junior School

Anger Is . . .

An evil elephant charging at me . . .
An angry lion roaring at me . . .
A spiteful teacher getting really cross.

Grace Unwin (8)
Church Crookham Junior School

Love

Love is when
You fall for someone,
When you have someone to hold,
When you have a soulmate for life.

Love is when
You find someone,
When you feel their pain,
When they feel yours.

Love is when
You feel your heart beating wildly
And you hear theirs,
Two people together forever.

Love is when
You feel they are there.
Even when they are gone
You can feel them by your side,
Forever and ever,
And that is love.

Samantha Dunn (10)
Church Crookham Junior School

In The Gloomy Forest

In the dark, dark forest
You might find bears in caves.
If you find one you'll get eaten.
In the dark, dark forest
You need a torch to see
Where you are going.
You might trip over
In the dark, dark forest.
That's why you don't go
In the dark, dark forest at night.
In the dark, dark forest.

Kirsty Bradley (9)
Church Crookham Junior School

Emotions

Shy is when you swallow your confidence,
It washes away like the sea
Tiptoeing in and out of the beach,
Bottling it all up.

Anger is a volcano about to erupt,
Throwing hot magma around,
As red as a tomato,
As hot as fire.

Excitement makes you feel curly,
It makes you feel dizzy and whizzy.
Excitement is colourful,
Like a twirly whirlpool.

Happiness is bright,
A wonderful sight.
You feel good inside,
You want to jump and shout.

Megan Reece (11)
Church Crookham Junior School

Love Is . . .

Love is gold like a solid ring.
Love is yellow like the bright sun.

Love feels like a leather bear.
Love feels like a smooth baby's bottom.

Love sounds like gentle music.
Love sounds like the gentle wind.

Love smells like delicious pink chocolate.
Love smells like a hamster nibbling.

Love makes me feel like a candle burning.
Love makes me feel like a baby dog.

Amber Lloyd (8)
Church Crookham Junior School

Anger

Anger is a red-hot chilli
Burning the roof
Of my mouth.

Anger is orange like a
Fierce, exploding volcano
Bubbling hot magma inside me.

Anger is a dark green tree,
Swerving from
Side to side.

Anger is ginger like a cat
Scratching a post
Smoothly.

Anger is grey like an elephant
Walking through
Different places.

Matthew Knock (10)
Church Crookham Junior School

Hunger Is . . .

Hunger is your tummy rumbling, about to erupt . . .
Friendly, fun food about to be eaten . . .
Plain, white chocolate as soft as cloth . . .
Driving to McDonald's with a pain in your tummy.

Joe Elliott (9)
Church Crookham Junior School

Fun Is . . .

The glowing sun shining on the sea . . .
Planting pretty plants in pots . . .
Like eating chocolate that melts in the mouth . . .
A trip to the park with my family.

Emily Harris (9)
Church Crookham Junior School

The Night Car

The night car stalks
Through the night
But in the morning
He's lifeless again.

He has night vision
Through his headlights
So nobody sees him
In the darkness.

He orders the traffic
To have a collision
In the dead of night,

And you can hear the roar
In the lonely night . . .
And watch out
For the bite.

Robert Earls (10)
Church Crookham Junior School

Darkness Is . . .

A dark, dull shadow in the corner . . .
A broken streetlight slowly flickering . . .
Like a road with no streetlights . . .
A car with broken headlights.

Lewis Charlie Moore (9)
Church Crookham Junior School

Hunger Is . . .

A fiery bomb in a stomach . . .
Horrible hidings going *rumble* . . .
As nasty as a fly . . .
Breathing with no air.

Imogen Frances Read (9)
Church Crookham Junior School

Love

Love is red like a beautiful rose.
Love smells like a fume of lavender.
Love tastes like calm blood.
Love reminds me of pink marshmallows.

Love sounds like a distant drum.
Love feels warm and everlasting.
Warm and everlasting,
Warm and everlasting.

Ryan Williams (9)
Church Crookham Junior School

Love

My hands clutch crimson roses
As my heart's beating inside of me
Like the Devil raging out of me.
I taste the sweetness of sugar
Dissolving on my tongue,
I smell the nectar from the roses
As the birds sing the sweet melody
That they do.

Cameo Louise Lang (11)
Church Crookham Junior School

My Emotions

Happiness is as colourful as a picture.
Anger is a volcano bursting out of you.
Love is smelling a crimson-red rose.
Loneliness is nothing - you don't want it -
Nothing at all . . .

Savannah Buckle (10)
Church Crookham Junior School

I Should Like To Paint . . .

I should like to paint . . .
A slithering snake,
A dinosaur doing a dance,
A counting cat collecting coins
And a dead dingbat doing a dare.

I should like to paint the sound of . . .
A whistling whale,
A shouting spider,
Some wishing well water,
And a creepy crash-test caterpillar.

I should like to paint the touch of . . .
A soft-skinned hamster,
A fluffy fish,
A frowning firebird
And a cute, cuddly cat.

Georgia Sheepwash (9)
Church Crookham Junior School

Fear

Fear is black, fiery
And fights just to fright.
Like a ghost wondering what to do next,
They're so scared, they flick off both of their shoes.
They're so scared, they partner up in twos.
They're so scared, they talk terribly.
They're so scared, they wish they never saw me.
They're so very scared, they pull out every one of their hairs.

Michael Colfer (8)
Church Crookham Junior School

Nervous!

When I'm feeling nervous
My stomach feels all funny
And my face turns as red
As a bowl full of chillies.

When I'm feeling nervous
I really want to cry
And nothing will make me feel better,
Not even apple pie.

When I'm feeling nervous
My eyes go all watery
And my mouth goes all sore.
My nose goes all runny
And when I speak, it sounds poor.

I hate feeling nervous,
I know you do too.
If only nervous wasn't a feeling at all,
The world would be really cool.

Chloe Eloise Jackson (10)
Church Crookham Junior School

Anger

Anger is like a parasite crawling inside you.
Anger is a rage flowing through you.
Anger tastes like a slimy slug.
Anger smells like a burning oil tank.
Anger looks like a ghost.
Anger reminds me of hatred.

Jamie Bailey (9)
Church Crookham Junior School

The Lonely Soldier

On the hills the dead men lie
And in the sky the larks still fly.
In no-man's-land wounded scream.
My family is dead, no one cares,
No one will know if I live or if I die.
My friends live no more
And in the trench the foul rats gnaw.
If I die then to Heaven I go.

Alexander Higgins (10)
Church Crookham Junior School

Spook - Mystery

Mystery is black like the dark.
It sounds like crickets rustling.
It smells like a cold breeze.
It looks pitch-black.
It feels like being watched.
It reminds me of going to your bedroom in the dark.

Ella Boulton (7)
Church Crookham Junior School

Silence Is . . .

Like living lifelessly in a world with no ears . . .
Sleeping soundlessly in a comfy warm bed
As quiet as a mouse . . .
Deep blue seas calming floating by
Not seeping one small sound.

Katie Rose Deans (9)
Church Crookham Junior School

Different

Happiness is like a giant star all blazing and hot.
Happiness is a true thing that stays put forever.
Happiness is a loud voice that flows through imagination.
Happiness feels like a very soft blanket.
Happiness tastes like a piece of your favourite food.
Happiness reminds me about true things that happen
                                  throughout your life.
Happiness is a scent of warm air from a tropical beach.
Happiness zooms through the world from every person.

Sadness is like a horrible giant stomping wherever he can.
Sadness is a droopy monster crying all over.
Sadness feels like a bumpy child dying of an illness.
Sadness tastes like baking, hot chilli.
Sadness reminds me of something bad.
Sadness sounds like nothing.
Sadness lives in an empty cave.
Sadness *is* nothing.

Thomas Edwards (9)
Church Crookham Junior School

When You Ride Your Bike

When you ride your bike, you will see a tree giving you oxygen,
And then you see a mummy bird giving her little ones food.
When you come to a zebra crossing you will see a car
Stopping to let you go across.
Then you can find sweets in the shop.
Then you go back home and you can see everything
You saw on your way there.
When you get back home you can make dinner,
Have your sweets and go to bed.

Callum Mercer (9)
Church Crookham Junior School

Feelings!

Happiness is blue like the air blowing through you.
Happiness is green like the cars zooming past.
Happiness is like a mountain of hot pizza.
Happiness is like chocolate melting on a hot day.
Happiness is like a dolphin diving in the sea.
Happiness is like a pony galloping along the sand.

Sadness is red like a blood sea.
Sadness is like a shark eating a human.
Sadness is like a human eating snails.
Sadness is like when you are feeling down.
Sadness is like a big, drippy nose.
Sadness is like a spider crawling up your leg.

Phoebe Robinson (9)
Church Crookham Junior School

Happiness

Happiness is yellow like the beautiful sun shining bright.
Happiness reminds me of when I went on a fabulous holiday.
Happiness looks like a lot of friendship.
Happiness sounds like lots of fun and laughter.
Happiness tastes like pizza.

Gemma Burge (9)
Church Crookham Junior School

Darkness Is . . .

A demand coming from an unknown planet . . .
The opposite of a happy hippo in the mud . . .
As dark and scary as someone in a Hallowe'en costume . . .
Making children still as a statue, trying not to move.

Annie Rose James (8)
Church Crookham Junior School

Anger!

Anger is black like a dead blackberry hanging on a branch.
Anger smells like gas.
Anger sounds like people shouting at you in your head.
Anger reminds me of when my rabbits died.
Anger tastes like black, burnt toast.
Anger is like a fierce lion.
Anger looks like burning fire.
Anger feels angry!

George Davis (8)
Church Crookham Junior School

Laughter is . . .

People loudly, lovingly laughing at me!
Me, laughing like a sly, naughty hyena!
Similar to a loud horn being blown repetitively.

Someone happy, swinging on a swing . . .
Like anyone opening their first birthday present . . .
A colourful rainbow hovering over my head.

Olivia McKeon (9)
Church Crookham Junior School

Fun Is . . .

The blazing, boiling sun . . .
Like dazzling diamonds, glittering gold . . .
Time for an ice cream!
Hearing the joyful cries of kids on a slide . . .
The 'Yay!' of a triumphant football team . . .
Enjoying the wonderful world.

Cameron Higgins (8)
Church Crookham Junior School

Emotions!

Anger is like a volcano erupting in my face.
Fear is like a wall trapping you every day.
Love is like a house with love hearts on the floor.
Happiness is like a friend helping and playing with you.
Sadness is like rain coming down from Heaven.
Loneliness is like a dark room with only you in it.
Hate is like a fire around you.
Anger, fear, love, happiness, loneliness and hate
Can be anything in the world to you and me.

Michaela Child (10)
Church Crookham Junior School

Happiness Is . . .

Beating my sister on the games console . . .
Eating Christmas crusty cake . . .
Playing football with my friends . . .
Going to the beach to see the surfy sand . . .
Telling spooky stories around the campfire.

Daniel Pesquero (9)
Church Crookham Junior School

Sadness Is . . .

Sadness is like ice-cold wind . . .
A wet tissue, cold and puffed . . .
A dark corridor with no end . . .
A brown dog looking very sad . . .
And being bad.

Matthew Swan (8)
Church Crookham Junior School

Death

Death is an empty room,
Not one single boom.
Darkness stalks you everywhere,
Nightmares are too much to bear.

A piece of puzzle missing - it's left a hole,
And feels like you've just sold your soul.
You've been cursed,
It's the Devil's worst.

A cloak of nothingness spreads over me,
I am not where I want to be.
Never-ending darkness, not a star twinkling,
I think I am sinking.

I don't want to live.
Is this what death does?

Chloe Davies (10)
Church Crookham Junior School

Love

Love feels like death at first,
Then it is like you are sitting
In a comfy chair.

Love looks like birds
Feeding their young
And horses galloping gallantly.

Love tastes like
Lipstick on your lips
And a glass of red wine.

Love smells like
Posh perfume in the air.
Love can tear us apart.

Jake Francis (10)
Church Crookham Junior School

Fear

Fear tastes like bitter lemon,
Making you wince as it touches your tongue.

Fear smells like fresh blood
Dripping onto the floor,
Staining the carpet as it goes.

Fear looks like a volcano erupting,
The lava creeping towards your feet
Like a snake stalking its prey.

Fear sounds like the scream of a girl
As her closet door opens in the night.

Fear feels like an earthquake,
The hole in the ground just waiting
To swallow you up for evermore.

Fear reminds you of death,
The dark wooden coffin
Buried, never to rise again.

Jonathan Hillson (11)
Church Crookham Junior School

Adventure

Adventure is a burst of excitement,
Like new places to explore.
It sounds like a brilliant new place
That people will love
And it smells like a brilliant new discovery.
It looks like an exciting place to be.
It feels like a new place about to burst
Out of a wonderful place.

Declan Downey (8)
Church Crookham Junior School

Goodbye

I say goodbye to all my fellows that lie,
It's like a bad dream that won't go away.
All I hear is 'Help, help' coming from the stars above,
It makes me feel like a lion has just attacked
My friend and I saw it happen.

I see a person dying in my arms.
It feels like a prickly bush that has just hit me.
It will always remind me of a gunshot
And someone dying on the floor.
I will never forget him!

I feel like I am in a prison with no way out.
Will I ever see him again?
He was my hero!

Olivia Rideout (10)
Church Crookham Junior School

Love Is . . .

A birthday present . . .
Like a fluffy pillow.
A lovely, lovely love heart given to me,
A box of chocolate given to me.
Like a red, rosy poppy.

Chloe McDonald (8)
Church Crookham Junior School

Happiness Is . . .

Pink fluffy cats posing at me . . .
A purple, pretty pillow waiting for me . . .
As fun as going out with my mates . . .
Like a home-made roast chicken . . .
Seeing my favourite family.

Sian Hundley (8)
Church Crookham Junior School

Fear

Fear tastes like an ice cube on your tongue.
Fear tastes like a frozen lake.

Fear smells like frozen white powder.
Fear smells like a black iced cake.

Fear looks like a bad dream haunting you for a long time.
Fear looks like a person fallen down onto rocks.

Fear feels like World War II.
Fear feels like dying.

Fear sounds like pounding drums.
Fear sounds like . . .

Kieran Sheepwash (11)
Church Crookham Junior School

Adventure

Adventure is yellow like a bright, big, curved banana.
It sounds like a terrifying monster quietly walking round the corner.
It smells like waves rushing to the shore in the breeze.
It looks like a terrifying tarantula creeping up the path.
It feels like excitement filling my strong muscles.
It reminds me of falling off my bunk bed.

Jamie Mullin (8)
Church Crookham Junior School

Mystery

A mystery is petrifying, like two eyes watching me.
It sounds like wind howling through the night.
It smells like a raging fire with flames like the sun.
It looks like a dark cave echoing in the darkness.
It feels like the sun setting my lips on fire.
It reminds me of the night I heard howling in the fog.

Sophie Cairns (7)
Church Crookham Junior School

Angry

Burnt chips sizzling in a pan,
Flaming fires burning wood,
Raging bulls running at you,
Pots of boiling water,
Bombs exploding.

Smelling mouldy cheese,
Car fuel stinking out the town,
Volcanoes spilling out lots of lava,
A bad day you don't want to happen,
Thunder and lightning going off near you.

Something bitter and sweet,
Fiery, hot chilli peppers stinging your mouth,
A bad dream that won't go away.

Soon anger becomes fear
That you can't run away from.

Zoe Westwood (11)
Church Crookham Junior School

Fear!

Chests pounding, waiting to escape from fear.
Creaking trees, cheering for fear.
Wind blowing, dancing for fear.
Dark alleys, with the mark of fear.
Swinging swings, calling for fear.
Flashing streetlamps, blinking at fear.
People shaking, in the presence of fear.
Temperature falling, at the sight of fear.
A large shadow creeping up behind you, when you hear fear.
The smell of burning, when you're near fear.
The smell of danger, as you charge at fear.
The smell of nothing, as you are sucked into fear.

Fear will do what fear does best,
Boo!

Grace Mayhew (10)
Church Crookham Junior School

Anger

Anger is something you never want to see.
Anger is something between you and me.

Anger is when you lose your best friend.
Anger is when your grandpa dies . . . and you feel alone.

Anger is something you never want to see.
Anger is something between you and me.

Anger is a fist wanting to punch.
Anger is a raging bull charging at the red cape held by the
                                        golden-dressed matador.

Anger is something you never want to see.
Anger is something between you and me.

Anger is hatred, anger is strong,
Anger is wrong.

Oliver Bainbridge (10)
Church Crookham Junior School

Adventure

Adventure is amazing like fireworks sizzling in the sky.
It sounds like leaves rustling in the wind.
It smells of discovery, like digging up a fossil.
It looks like autumn and the leaves are on the ground.
It feels like I am in a storybook full of magical adventures.

Thomas Potter (7)
Church Crookham Junior School

Friendliness

Friendliness is blue like the sky.
Friendliness tastes like pizza.
Friendliness feels like smooth spheres.
Friendliness sounds like hip hop music.

James King (9)
Church Crookham Junior School

Loneliness

Loneliness is when you're on your own.
Loneliness feels like a river with no fish in it.
Loneliness tastes like nothing, nothing at all.
Loneliness smells like burnt chips on a summer's day.
Loneliness looks like some friends breaking apart, falling out.
Loneliness sounds like wind sweeping along the ground,
                                        blowing the leaves around.

Grace Young (10)
Church Crookham Junior School

Adventure

Adventure is something new that you've never done in your life
Like going to a new country.
It sounds like roaring aeroplanes in the sky.
It smells like delicious fish and chips.
It looks like scaly lizards in the sun.
It feels like crumbling sand between my toes.
It reminds me of the beach on a hot day.

Sam Killick (7)
Church Crookham Junior School

Adventure

Adventure is great like treasure,
It sounds like laughter,
It looks like a pool of money,
It feels like the warm blue sea,
It reminds me of happy memories.

Adam Crumpton (7)
Church Crookham Junior School

Adventure

Adventure is exciting like an alien walking through a forest
in a thunderstorm!
It sounds like an animal on Mars.
It smells like a cheetah's dinner that has gone off!
It looks like an odd plant in the imperial galaxy!
It feels like a slob that I don't want to eat.
It reminds me of my favourite time!

Adam Bolton (7)
Church Crookham Junior School

Love

Love is red like a red rose.
It tastes like my first kiss.
It feels like my mum and dad when we hug.
It reminds me of someone's marriage.
It smells like me when I cosy up and watch a DVD.
It looks like a lovely love heart.

Dominic Leigh Horton (9)
Church Crookham Junior School

Anger

Anger is a raging bull running through a china shop.
Anger is a volcano that is ready to explode.
Anger is the bittersweet taste creeping to the tip of my tongue.
Anger is a snake trying to escape.
Then when the anger reaches the top - *bang!*

Caitlin Davis (10)
Church Crookham Junior School

Adventure

Adventure is blue like the deep sea.
It sounds like waves crashing against rocks.
It smells like disgusting salty water.
It looks like the sun blazing across the water.
It feels like sand rushing through my hands.
It reminds me of when a crab bit me.

Mark Walter (7)
Church Crookham Junior School

Mystery

Mystery is black like the blackness of my shadow.
It sounds like sizzling water coming up the stairs.
It smells like a haunted hamburger coming to get me.
It looks like fiery smoke coming under my door.
It feels like hot, burning water flowing after me.
It reminds me of when I ran so fast I ran into a tree.

Oliver Sanderson (7)
Church Crookham Junior School

Adventure

Adventure is black like the night with no light.
It sounds like vampires' sucking blood.
It smells like blood.
It looks like vampires floating around.
It feels like vampires coming towards me.
It reminds me of falling into the sea.

Caitlin Stewart (7)
Church Crookham Junior School

Adventure

Adventure is blue like the sea and the sky.
It sounds like a ghost creeping about.
It smells like a fire spreading about.
It looks like a dark sky covering a city.
It feels like a burning fire tearing a house apart.
It reminds me of when my dad's bunny ran into a tree.

William Lloyd (7)
Church Crookham Junior School

Mystery

Mystery is black like the shadow of my bedroom.
It sounds like a paid assassin creeping towards me.
It smells like the blood of a Siberian wolf's teeth.
It looks like a Minotaur creeping for me.
It feels like an anaconda slithering through my hands.
It reminds me of a graveyard where soon I will die.

Matthew Fordham (8)
Church Crookham Junior School

Darkness

Darkness is black like night with no stars or a moon.
It tastes like a poisonous medicine.
It sounds like a ghost hooting in the moonlight.
It reminds me of people trick or treating at Hallowe'en.
It feels like vampires' teeth moving into my body.
That is darkness.

Matthew Tyler (10)
Church Crookham Junior School

Love Is . . .

Love is red like a bleeding heart that never stops beating.
It feels like chocolate melting in my mouth.
It sounds like birds singing in the clear blue sky.
It smells like scented perfume sprayed on soft skin.
It tastes like sweet, sweet candyfloss being sold at a sweet stall
                                                                                         in a park.
It reminds me of beautiful flowers on a sunny day.

Sophie Ellis (10)
Church Crookham Junior School

Anger

Anger is red like a burst of fire.
Anger reminds me of death and destruction.
Anger tastes like red-hot chillies.
Anger smells like burning tyres.
Anger sounds like a falling rockslide.
Anger feels like burning metals resting on my head.

Peter Bolton (10)
Church Crookham Junior School

Love Is Like

Love is pink like fluffy candyfloss.
It tastes like marshmallows dipped in chocolate sauce.
It feels like love hearts rubbing against your lips
And smells like strawberry shampoo-covered hair.
That is what love is like.

Alastair Lee (10)
Church Crookham Junior School

Adventure

Adventure is exciting new things,
Like things you've never done.
It sounds like rustling, scared thoughts in your head.
It smells like evil darkness.
It looks like good, new things.
It feels like the coldness of the North Pole.
It reminds me of the brightness of sunlight.

Jamie House (7)
Church Crookham Junior School

Fear

Fear is like a big ghost watching me.
It smells like fire behind me.
It tastes like blood in my mouth.
It feels like a car running me over.
It sounds like someone screaming for help.
It reminds me of me dying.

Becky Wall (9)
Church Crookham Junior School

Mystery

Mystery is frightful like evil ghosts.
It sounds like howling wolves in the night.
It smells like rotten fruits on the green floor.
It looks like thirsty vampires sucking blood.
It feels like sticky goo running through my fingers.
It reminds me of spooky monsters coming to eat us all!

Bethany Middleton (8)
Church Crookham Junior School

Adventure

Adventure is monsters glowing through the forest
Like they want to eat you!
It sounds like bears scratching the bark off the trees.
It smells like thick, gooey cream.
It looks like the moon shining down on you!
It feels like sloppy ice cream.
It reminds me of falling in a river.

Madi Bate (7)
Church Crookham Junior School

Mystery

Mystery is creepy like a big spider.
It sounds like a cool breeze rustling through the branches.
It smells like smoke from the campfire.
It looks like beautiful flowers in the spring.
It feels like it's summer already.
It reminds me of Easter when everybody's really cheerful.

Megan Price (8)
Church Crookham Junior School

Adventure

Adventure is different, like whistling of the wind.
It smells like the bark of the old trees.
It looks like a rearing horse.
It feels like a soft cushion.
It reminds me of a polar bear.

Jasmine Price (8)
Church Crookham Junior School

Adventure

Adventure is superb because you can discover lots of things
Like elephant can hear from long distances.
It sounds like birds swooping and singing
Gorgeously through the air.
It smells like beautiful sky floating to the wild.
It looks like clouds moving around the world.
It feels like surprise coming into your body.
It reminds me of the sun appearing and disappearing.

Gemma Morgan (8)
Church Crookham Junior School

Adventure

Adventure is purple like a crocus swaying in the wind.
It sounds like a fairy playing in the green grass.
It smells like a beautiful heather.
It looks like a colourful rainbow.
It feels like a smooth rock.
It reminds me of a pot of gold.

Emily McCulloch (8)
Church Crookham Junior School

Adventure

Adventure is like yellow sun coming to my eyes.
It sounds like rushing waves coming to my boat.
It smells like salty water.
It feels like rain dripping on me.
It reminds me of splashing in the sea.

Bethan Davies (7)
Church Crookham Junior School

Adventure

Adventure is exciting, like when you find
The first thing that you were looking for.
It sounds like a very noisy play park.
It smells like really yummy cake.
It looks like three million heads on a monster.
It feels like slimy and rough skin.
It reminds me of scary ogres and ugly ogres.

Thomas Vickery (7)
Church Crookham Junior School

Adventure

An adventure is amazing, like a big surprise.
It sounds like a noisy playground.
It smells like my favourite food.
It looks pretty like a princess.
It feels like discovery.
It reminds me of me.

Douglas Critchley (8)
Church Crookham Junior School

Adventure

Adventure is amazing, like in a rainforest
It sounds like the wind is windy.
It smells like bark on the tree.
It looks like the sun is shining brightly.
It feels like it is a new world
It reminds me of a great day.

Lili Swain (8)
Church Crookham Junior School

Sadness Is Round Every Corner

Sadness is like the white snow,
You never know when it will stop or start.
Sadness smells like a white orchid.
Sadness feels like being stabbed in the back.
Sadness tastes like the salty sea.
Sadness reminds me of my cat that died
On the 11th January 2008, aged 18 (our years).

Joe Hutton (10)
Church Crookham Junior School

Love

Love is pink like a blooming flower.
Love tastes like my mum kissing me.
Love feels like a glistening fire.
Love sounds like my heart beating frantically.
Love smells like marshmallows over the fire.
Love reminds me of walking on the beach.

Charlie Crumpton (9)
Church Crookham Junior School

Happiness

Happiness is white like a blanket of snow.
It tastes like hot chocolate running down my throat.
It feels like soft puppy's fur brushing my hand
It smells like roasting marshmallows round the campfire.
It reminds me of the time I went on holiday, having lots of fun.

Holly Geall (9)
Church Crookham Junior School

Hate

Hate is black like the dark clouds in the sky.
Hate sounds like someone is yelling at me.
Hate feels like a ball of fire inside me.
Hate smells like a fire burning hard wood.
Hate tastes like a fire burning in my mouth.
Hate reminds me of someone annoying me.

Tiegan Skinner (9)
Church Crookham Junior School

Happiness Around

Happiness is blue like dolphins splashing in the sea.
It tastes like sweet, tender ice cream.
It feels like children laughing happily.
It smells like lavender floating around the air.
It reminds me of fun times with my grandad.

Daniel Gray (10)
Church Crookham Junior School

Love

Love is pink like soft candyfloss.
Love feels like flying through the sky.
Love reminds me of fluffy hearts.
Love sounds like your heart beating inside you.
Love tastes like soft, squishy marshmallows.

Daniel Campbell (10)
Church Crookham Junior School

Happiness

Happiness is blue like the sky on a sunny summer's day.
It smells like lavender wafting under my nose.
It tastes like creamy chocolate cake with sprinkles on the top.
It sounds like people laughing on a hot summer's day.
It feels like a warm wind blowing on my face.
It reminds me of my friends being funny, and their cute laughs.

Alexandra Laing (9)
Church Crookham Junior School

Love

Love is pink like a soft and sticky marshmallow.
Love tastes like sweet candyfloss.
Love feels like a soft, clean pillow.
Love sounds like tweeting blue tits in a tree.
Love smells like tangy rosemary from the garden.
Love reminds me of soft flowers in a meadow.

Helen Walter (9)
Church Crookham Junior School

Sadness

Sadness is black like a droopy, wet, cold day.
It reminds me of when my real dad died.
It smells like a dark midnight without a moon.
It tastes like a heart broken into bite-sized pieces.
It sounds like someone crying for help.

Travis Milton (9)
Church Crookham Junior School

Anger

Anger tastes like roast chicken that's been in an oven.
It feels like the hot, boiling sun.
It sounds like the car's tyres screeching around like a bull.
Anger reminds me of a mad bull breathing heavily
With air coming out like a volcano ready to erupt.
It smells like a shark's blood pouring out like a waterfall,
Speeding down like a car travelling at 500 miles per hour.
It looks like a volcano coming up on the mountain.

Semiti Marautaki (9)
Church Crookham Junior School

Happiness

Happiness is yellow like the bright shining sun.
Happiness sounds like children playing all around me.
Happiness smells like the scent of warm air.
Happiness tastes like eating creamy ice cream.
Happiness looks like some chocolate melting in my hands.
Happiness reminds you of eating lots of chocolate.

Ellis Hardy (9)
Church Crookham Junior School

Anger

Anger is red like a blazing fire.
It tastes like rotten food at the back of the cupboard.
It feels like prickly spikes stuck to me and my clothes.
It sounds like Mum shouting at me.
It reminds me of getting angry with my sis.

Thomas Davies (9)
Church Crookham Junior School

Happiness

Happiness is light blue like families in the park.
Happiness tastes like rosy-red strawberries.
Happiness sounds like birds tweeting in the tree.
Happiness feels like me and my friends playing at the funfair,
And when you touch a smooth page in my book.
Happiness looks like families at Christmas eating their dinner.
Happiness smells like pretty flowers looking at me.
Happiness reminds me of Christmas time
When children open their presents.

Vicki Lee Duemke (9)
Church Crookham Junior School

Fear

Fear is white like a bolt of lightning.
It smells like a dark corner of an alleyway.
It sounds like chattering of perfect teeth.
It feels like ferocious wolves tearing me limb from limb.
It reminds me of when my golden puppy got taken away.

Robert Colfer (10)
Church Crookham Junior School

Darkness

Darkness is black like a frosty night sky.
Darkness sounds like the howling wind rushing through the trees.
Darkness feels like ice cubes sliding down my neck.
Darkness reminds me of ghosts glistening in the moon.
Darkness tastes like cold ice cream slipping down your throat.

Hannah Neil (9)
Church Crookham Junior School

Excitement

Excitement is as gold as the glittering golden sun.
Excitement tastes like fizzing, bubbling lemonade.
Excitement feels like rainbow-coloured fireworks popping in
my body.
Excitement sounds like a shooting star zooming past.
Excitement smells like popping popcorn in a boiling oven.
Excitement looks like my sister's crazy hair.
Excitement reminds me of my friends and my band, the
'White Angels'.

Megan Benson (9)
Church Crookham Junior School

Happiness Hope

Hope tastes like a yummy chocolate bar melting in my mouth.
Hope sounds like birds tweeting nice and softly.
Hope feels like a rough, bouncy trampoline bouncing high.
Hope smells like a red rose blowing in the cold breeze.
Hope looks like two friends together.
Hope reminds me of a sunny, warm holiday at the beach.

Courtney Louise Chilvers (8)
Church Crookham Junior School

Laughter

Laugher is multicoloured like a rainbow.
It tastes like Maltesers crunching in my mouth.
It feels like being at a seaside, having fun.
Laughter sounds like a band playing lovely music.
It smells like a group of flowers swooshing side to side.
It reminds me of playing with my friends.

Marina Fedoroff (9)
Church Crookham Junior School

Happiness

Happiness is pink like candyfloss.
Happiness tastes like soft sugar sprinkled on top of sweets.
It looks like friendship going on outside.
It reminds me of Christmas with paper getting ripped.
Happiness is families spending time together.
It feels like rainbows appearing from nowhere.
It smells like roses opening bright.
It sounds like a discussion ready for tonight.

Chelsie Gray (9)
Church Crookham Junior School

Fun

Fun is a rainbow of colours like glistening gold in the sun.
It tastes like friendship, kindness, happiness, excitement
                                            and laughter.
It feels like butterflies fluttering in the breeze.
It smells like sweet-scented flowers and fizzy lemonade.
It sounds like children playing football and dazzling birds flying past.
It looks like a feathery eagle swooping down to its twiggy nest.
It reminds me of boiled sweets being shared out.

Lauren Vickery (8)
Church Crookham Junior School

Love

Love is blue like Hannah's school jumper.
It tastes like strawberries with sugar, it is very sweet.
It feels like a sponge washing a motorbike.
It reminds me of Michael's first birthday.
It sounds like a bird being shot down.

James Burrell (8)
Church Crookham Junior School

Hunger

Hunger is green like the bright grass.
It tastes like a lovely bowl of pasta.
Hunger looks like a delicious plate of chicken.
It sounds like a rumble in the jungle.
Hunger reminds me of when I was a cute, crying baby.
It feels like a squidgy rubber covered in water.
Hunger smells like a barbecue when the sausages are grilled.
Hunger hurts my tummy.
Hunger!

Hannah Phillipou (9)
Church Crookham Junior School

Anger

Anger is the colour black when you're feeling mad at someone.
It tastes like a football in mud.
It feels like soil crumbling in my hands.
It smells like the dirty rubbish bin.
It sounds like somebody shouting.
It looks like a wrecked book.
It reminds me of a dark dungeon.

Joshua Atkinson (9)
Church Crookham Junior School

Adventure

Adventure is green like a fresh and cool fern hanging from a tree.
It sounds like some insects flying smoothly up and down.
It smells like the sun burning on you.
It feels like the rain pitter-pattering on your arm.
It reminds me of having fun and amazing discoveries.

Eleanor Hobby (8)
Church Crookham Junior School

Jealous

Jealous is dark green like a green bottle being smashed.
It tastes like a lot of bubbles bubbling with fury.
When you are jealous it sounds like someone teasing you.
Jealous smells like horse manure being thrown at you!
Jealous makes you feel anger and you want what they've got,
　　　　　　　　　　　　　　　　you feel you need it.
Jealous looks like a big black hole in space.
Jealous reminds me of a best friend break up.

Connie Margaret Rolls (9)
Church Crookham Junior School

Darkness

Darkness is black like a dark thunderstorm.
Darkness smells like a pitch-black tornado zooming around my room.
Darkness looks like a beautiful black cat.
Darkness sounds like a zooming whirlpool racing round and round.
Darkness tastes like blackberries melting in my mouth.
Darkness reminds me of a dark summer's night.
Darkness feels like a giant foot stepping on me.

Katie Wakelin (9)
Church Crookham Junior School

Love

The colour of love is pink like a rose.
It tastes like the first time I had KFC.
It looks like a lovely love heart.
It smells like KFC.
It sounds like music to my ears.
It reminds me of my first kiss.

Nathan Charles Kingham (9)
Church Crookham Junior School

Broken Hearts

Love is red like broken hearts
Flying all over the world.
It tastes like mouldy food
That I can't stop eating.

Love looks like a broken leg
That can't be fixed.
It sounds like a musical wedding
That you weren't invited to.

Love looks like your boyfriend
Marrying someone else.
It smells like a cigarette
That everybody is using.

Love reminds me of my boyfriend
Who loves me.

Bethany Louise Gray (8)
Church Crookham Junior School

Love

Love is as red as a soft-petalled rose.
Love tastes like a juicy strawberry.
It reminds me of my family.
It smells like perfume.
It looks like my friends
And it sounds like my mum saying goodnight.

Shaun Kern (8)
Church Crookham Junior School

Happiness

Happiness is orange like the sun.
Happiness tastes like vanilla ice cream.
Happiness feels like fluffy, soft pillows.
Happiness sounds like pop music.

John Roome (9)
Church Crookham Junior School

Emotions

I am purple with loneliness
Like a little bee all alone,
No one around me,
So quiet you could even hear a tiny moan.

I am blue with relaxation,
Like a tired lion cub falling asleep,
Just waiting for the alarm clock to wake me up,
Until it goes *beep*.

I am white with shyness,
Like a little bunny hiding in a bush,
Scared away from the stranger
Who looks like he wants to give me a push.

I am yellow with excitement,
Like a playful bear cub,
Jumping up and down,
Waiting for the moment I am excited for.

Siân Roberts (10)
Church Crookham Junior School

The Light In Your Life

The light in your life is a glowing gold smile
Like a shining star.
The light in your life is oozing,
Melting chocolate wafting very far.
The light in your life is a shining rainbow,
All colourful and bright.
The light in your life is a day at a blazing hot beach,
The sun giving light.
The light in your life is a bird's tune,
Tweeting in the magical sky.
The light in your life is your friends laughing,
Saying hello and goodbye.
The light in your life is . . . well you decide!

Keeley Ducker (11)
Church Crookham Junior School

Emotions

Sad is the black darkness blocking out the light
As it tries to reach past the cloud.
Sad is the dark, blue sea
Crashing against the rocks.

Happy is the bright, yellow sun
Beaming its mighty rays to everyone.
Happy are the green, healthy trees,
Swaying gently in the breeze.

Anger is the red blood in your veins
Waiting to burst out through your skin.
Anger is the orange lava in the volcano,
Burning the molten rock.

Relaxed is the purple flowers
You lie amongst in the meadow.
Relaxed is the light blue sky
High above the ground.

Jack Garvey (10)
Church Crookham Junior School

Jealousy

She seemed to have everything I could ever have wanted,
It made my blood boil to say her name,
I felt the volcano burning inside of me,
Waiting to erupt with a big loud bang.

She seemed to be everything I could ever have wanted,
It made me turn green when she got full marks.
When she always won prizes and got what she wanted,
I felt as if I was ready to burst.

She would go round boasting and hurting people's feelings,
Always making such a scene,
But as you get on with life, you learn to let them be.

Rebecca Consterdine (10)
Church Crookham Junior School

Emotions

Embarrassment is a red balloon
Getting bigger and bigger by the second.
Embarrassment is your head looking towards the ground
And knowing you've let yourself down.

Relaxed is a tropical island,
The sea breeze swaying in and out.
Relaxed is a bright green meadow,
Untouched and lazing in the sun.

Sad is a very dark cupboard
With someone sitting inside.
Sad is shut in a corner,
Away from all of mankind.

Anger is a jalapeno pepper,
Sharp and burning your mouth.
Anger is boiling hot magma
Erupting from the volcano inside.

Disappointed is your hopes becoming crushed,
Like a field being built over.
Disappointed is things you wish you had
And wanting them more than ever.

Confused is jumbled letters and numbers
Flowing through your head.
Confused is not knowing what to do,
You don't know where you belong.

Jack Chapman (10)
Church Crookham Junior School

Love

L ove is really funny
O r it feels that you can fly
V alentine is also love
E veryone loves someone.

Ugnius Zelba (11)
Oakridge Junior School

Love Versus Anger

Love,
Soft and gentle,
Passionate and secure,
It overtakes the lover's life,
Love.

Anger,
Fiery, strong,
Monstrous, livid thoughts
Control the beating heart and soul,
Anger.

Isobel Tennison (11)
Oakridge Junior School

Hatred

This isn't my fault.
I hate people, people hate me.
What is the world like?

Today this is Earth.
I hate the world and so does it,
This thing I can't help.

Joseph Clarke (9)
Oakridge Junior School

Feelings

Feelings,
Those of good cheer,
Your head above the clouds,
And those of sadness and envy
All around.

Connor O'Brien (10)
Oakridge Junior School

Egypt Poem

Sandy,
Summer,
A gold Heaven,
A sunny breeze,
A linen robe,
A pharaoh's throne,
A holiday advert,
A warm curry.

Zack Gill (7)
Oakridge Junior School

Egypt

Egypt is the colour gold
It is summer
It is a sandy beach
It is a sunshiny day
It is a warm cloak
It is a leather sofa
It is a black jackal
It is roast potatoes.

Paul Izzard (8)
Oakridge Junior School

Roses

Roses are dark red like the sun.
Roses are sweet like sugar.
Roses are attractive to people.
Roses are for Valentine's Day.
Roses are like red beetles.
Roses are just like you.

Cade Martin (8)
Oakridge Junior School

Happiness

H ugs when somebody's arms are tightly squeezed around my body
A ffectionate smiles that you feel in your heart
P assionate about life
P eaceful and calm
I n my own world surrounded by love
N ever have any horrible thoughts
E verlasting love that fills up inside
S imple as ABC is feeling happy
S trong as love has ever been.

Maisy McDonough-Dancer (10)
Oakridge Junior School

Feelings

F eelings, feelings everywhere
E veryone has feelings but some people just don't care
E verywhere there is a feeling
L ove, anger, all of these are feelings
I nside the heart is where the feeling comes from
N obody can have no feelings
G oing somewhere with a feeling always
S o feelings exist now and they always will.

Kelsey Mosquera (9)
Oakridge Junior School

Jolly

J umpy children that can't stop
O ld people who like to have fun
L ucky children that get lots of holidays
L ucky children that have a great family
Y ou and I have so much fun together.

Jessica Bridgeman (10)
Oakridge Junior School

Feelings

F eelings, feelings we have
E verywhere you can see feelings in you
E veryone does not care
L osing friends is upsetting
I ndividual is good
N o one likes me
G anging up on me is scary
S ulking in the corner all day long.

Lauren Paine (10)
Oakridge Junior School

Feelings

H ope is for a beautiful summer
O ptimistic feelings for life
P eace for today
E stablish your feelings
F lowers will start to grow if this is the world
U ndercover feelings will emerge
L ove is all of this.

Jessica Muller (10)
Oakridge Junior School

Feelings

J umping people that can't stop
O ld people that are having fun
L ucky children that get presents
L ively, maniac children that just can't calm down
Y ou just can't stop being jolly.

Kyra Wright (11)
Oakridge Junior School

Anger

A nger is like mad panting
N ever happy or proud
G ives grief to other people
E ither hurts somebody on the inside or the outside
R evealing the sadness of the person.

Chloe Brede (9)
Oakridge Junior School

Happiness

H appiness
A ll around
P urple, pink and red
P eople passionately living their lives
Y ellow, joyful, peaceful.

Sallyann Blanchard (11)
Oakridge Junior School

Love

L ove is a thing that I can see
O ut there is someone special for me
V ery good is how I feel
E very week a sundae and a meal.

Jasmin Lee (10)
Oakridge Junior School

Love

L ove is in the air
O ver the hill there is a pair of lovebirds
V iolins play as they fly
E ven through the hard times.

Melissa Gallop (9)
Oakridge Junior School

Sadness

S adness feels like being down in the dumps
A nd always left out
D efinitely when friends turn and walk away
N ever, ever be happy again
E very day as lonely as ever
S adness is so horrible
S adness is wrong.

Carah Newlands (11)
Oakridge Junior School

Jealousy

J ealousy bubbling inside
E asily overcomes pride
A rranging a horrible cunning plan
L anguages speaking loudly in my head
O f course over this feeling I'd rather be dead
U nbelievably selfish and terribly cruel
S ome stupid teenagers may think this feeling is cool
Y et I know it isn't at all.

Lauren-Rose Lambert (9)
Oakridge Junior School

Hatred

H atred is a horrible emotion
A ngry for revenge
T ired for love
R ed is the colour of hatred
E veryone hates
D espise and death.

Rhys Dawkins (10)
Oakridge Junior School

Feelings

F eelings are there
E verywhere
E veryone's got them
L ove is one
I ll is another
N ervous too
G uilty when you've done wrong
S o some are sad, some are happy.

George McRae (10)
Oakridge Junior School

Sad Bad Poem

S isters are annoying
A re girls bad?
D isturbing dogs

B oys are dead
A lways agree with me
D ead men RIP.

Shane Paterson (11)
Oakridge Junior School

Anger

A nger is powerful
N ever-ending
G ives you grief
E verybody hates you
R evealing the anger inside you.

Eleanor Jeffery (9)
Oakridge Junior School

Feelings

L ove is happy
O r it can be funny
V alentine's is love
E verybody needs love

H appy is nice
A ll people should be happy
P eople are sometimes
P eople are always happy
Y ou're supposed to be happy.

Luka Virgilio (9)
Oakridge Junior School

Feelings

H appy summers
O h please let it happen
P eace for the world
E legant love
F eeling happy
U ndercover love
L ove.

Rachel Bennett (10)
Oakridge Junior School

Love

L ove is everywhere
O r funny
V ery valuable
E veryone needs it.

Adam Richardson (10)
Oakridge Junior School

A Mummy

A mummy is as brown as a hedgehog.
A mummy is the season, spring.
A mummy is the place, Heaven.
A mummy is a wet storm.
A mummy is old bandages.
A mummy is a coffin.
A mummy is an Egyptian programme.
A mummy is a bar of chocolate.

Oliver Lucas (9)
Oakridge Junior School

Egypt

Egypt is a yellow place far, far away.
Egypt is a very, very hot place.
Egypt is a hot place very far away.
Egypt is well the hottest place in the world.
Egypt has got very soft clothing.
It is a camel watching a sunset in Egypt.
It is a basket of grapes.

Patrick Fastnedge (8)
Oakridge Junior School

Lovely Roses

Roses are light red as the hot sun.
Roses are like summer by the water.
Roses are like England.
Roses are like a cloak of gold.
Roses are like a red door.
Roses are like a ladybird.
Roses are like pearls of love.

Megan Orton (9)
Oakridge Junior School

Octopoem Egypt

The colour that matches is gold.
A hot day like summer fills the air with glee.
The country is like a sandy beach.
The gleaming sunshine glows down on us
Like a star in the night.
Soft silk sways from side to side.
Sarcophagus waiting inside a pyramid
For someone to be buried.
An ox ploughing in the mud.
A juicy fig waiting to be bought.

Lucy Smith (8)
Oakridge Junior School

Tigers

Tigers are bright orange, just like the sun.
They are like a beautiful summery day.
Tigers are like a big tropical rainforest.
They are like a glorious sunny day.
Tigers are like beautiful, orange, woolly jumpers.
They are like an orange, stripy rug.
Tigers are the most wonderful creatures in the world.
They are like a crispy, roast chicken with succulent bacon.

Georgia Bicknell (9)
Oakridge Junior School

Tombs

A tomb full of gold walls,
Buried on a boiling hot summer day
In Egypt with a cursed mummy inside,
With a boiling sun above it.
The men, wearing a small cloth, while burying the tomb.
A cat, Pharaoh's favourite animal.
Sweetcorn as gold as the tomb.

Holly McCann (8)
Oakridge Junior School

What I Think Of Egypt

Egypt is the bright colour of gold.
It is summer that is a hot, sticky season.
I see Egypt as a sandy yellow beach
With many people there.
It's a sunny, hot day, all sticky as the sandstorm.
Egypt is a linen cloak as women used to make.
Egypt is a big bed fit for a pharaoh.
It is Bastet, the cat god.
It is a pizza that just came out of the oven, yum!
That is Egypt!

Cally Pettifor (9)
Oakridge Junior School

Egypt

Egypt is a gold beach shimmering and shining in the sun.
It is summer and it is hot, where lizards crawl about.
Egypt is a place where palaces are.
It is hot and sunny there.
Egypt is a gold jumper.
Egypt is a gold, soft sofa.
It is a leopard running over the landscape.
It is a fish's skin shimmering in the water.

Dylan Jones (8)
Oakridge Junior School

My Father, Tutankhamun

My father, Tutankhamun, is gold as the sun.
Father is summer to me 'cause
He is bright as his gold crown.
My father is a place of golden jewels.
Father is a sunny, calm, beautiful day.
My father is a shining crown
Sitting on the royal pillow.

Kaaviya Rajapakeerathan (9)
Oakridge Junior School

A Place Where I Discover Egypt

A sandy-coloured country,
A hot summer's day,
A wonderful, wide, sandy beach,
A beautiful sunny day,
Soft cream homemade clothing made with care,
A cosy tomb waiting to rest in,
The holiday channel,
A yummy loaf of bread, mmm!
This is the country I discovered.

Georgia Harwood (8)
Oakridge Junior School

Tutankhamen

Tutankhamen is the colour of golden sand, lovely and gold.
Tutankhamen is summer.
He is a park,
He is a sunny day.
Tutankhamen looks like linen bandages.
He is a pharaoh's crown.
He is a yellow lion.
He is a lovely, tasty, bowl of chips.

Belle Wrangles (7)
Oakridge Junior School

Ancient Egypt

Egypt is as bright as gold.
Egypt is summer, so lovely and warm.
Egypt is a place where you
Have to work hard and never stop.
Egypt is hot, hot as an oven.

Chloe Flores (9)
Oakridge Junior School

Depressed

Depressed, nobody knows,
Curling up in my bed, sad,
The world against me.

My friends ask what's wrong,
I can't tell them, I don't know.
All alone, no one.

Unfamiliar,
Crying every day and night,
I want to be me.

Oris Shenyan (10)
Oakridge Junior School

Egypt

Egypt is sandy and yellow.
It is summer.
It is an everlasting beach.
It is a summer's day.
It is a white linen dress.
It is a pharaoh's throne.
It is a black jackal.
It is a turkey fresh from the oven.

Joshua Andrews (8)
Oakridge Junior School

Sadness

Every life is bad,
Some are better than others,
Make the most of it.

James Beeden (10)
Oakridge Junior School

The Oakridge Poem

Green,
It is spring.
It is a forest of learning.
It is a hot, summer day.
A green jumper.
It is a green, school chair.
It is a green budgie.
It is a can of baked beans.

Tommy Barkham (8)
Oakridge Junior School

Angry

I am very frustrated,
Not that happy,
Greatly angry with someone,
Regretting that he was my friend.
Why am I angry at the past?
Not attacked me again so far.
Suspecting a surprise attack.
Slithering like a slimy snake.

Nick Frazer (10)
Oakridge Junior School

Sorrow

S ad, so sad
O ld friends dying every day
R IP to them
R unning round my mind
O bviously I'm sad!
W hat I really want is them back alive!

Lorelei Nielsen (9)
Oakridge Junior School

Love Is Comfy

L ove is the world of marriage, rising on together
O ver the moon for someone, the vows last forever
V aluable gifts passed to each other
E venings spent together

I nterested in the same things
S pend life together

C omfort together every day
O ver the moon for someone
M other love is here
F ound when lost
Y et, over the moon with each other.

Joshua Blaber (10)
Oakridge Junior School

Feelings

F eelings come in different shapes and sizes
E veryone has lots of feelings
E very day you have a choice of feelings
L ive your life with the feelings you have
I hate having bad feelings
N ever do I want to feel sad
G ood feelings make me feel great
S ad feelings make me feel down in the dumps.

Philly Holden (10)
Oakridge Junior School

Feelings

Feeling sad or glad,
Feelings are all around us,
Fun, sad, great and mad.

Riley Fenn (9)
Oakridge Junior School

In Love

In love
Falling for you
Together forever
Valentine gifts for each other
In love.

Mary Roberts (11)
Oakridge Junior School

Love

L ove is over the hills
O ver the mountain tops
V iolets are growing to make love
E very day love is in the air.

Alex Downham (9)
Oakridge Junior School

War Feelings

Don't die,
Hold the fear in,
Lock it up, don't spill tears,
Keep on smiling, they'll be waiting,
Don't die!

Georgia Ariss (11)
Oakridge Junior School

Hate Poem

H ate is a horrible thing
A t its best it is irritating
T errible, terrible hate
E xcellent people think it's despicable.

Craig Niven (11)
Oakridge Junior School

Scared

S orrow, scared souls
C an't wait to get out
A lways being hurt
R eady to be let out
E ating up my heart
D eath is in my path.

Courtney Clement (10)
Oakridge Junior School

Silly

S illy thing in the air
I rritating things they don't care
L ittle nasty up and down
L ittle thing get a crown
Y ellow bug with a bug buzzing up and down.

Nicole Coyle (10)
Oakridge Junior School

Upset

U pset is not happiness
P retty feelings, sad feelings
S adly painful, upset friends
E ating nothing, down in the dumps,
T ears running, wet cheeks, upset is a feeling.

Lisa Bartlett (11)
Oakridge Junior School

Hatred

H ell ripping me apart
A ngry and horrible inside
T errorizing people all day
R evenge to the Devil
E ating everyone's heart
D estruction to the world.

Joseph Smith (10)
Oakridge Junior School

Happy

H ugs - kisses
A lways with you
P laying with your friends
P eople help you when you are hurt
Y ou love.

Sheyanne Tedford (9)
Oakridge Junior School

Happy Feelings

H appy feelings all around
A s happiness fills the ground
P eace and quiet
P layful people
Y ou and I will never cry.

Tegan Ledger (9)
Oakridge Junior School

Happy

H is for happiness, you are sensitive when you are happy
A nimals make you happy and sad sometimes
P arties make you a happy place and they make you happy because you get to invite your friends
P addling is happy because you are in the sea, swimming with your family
Y oghurts are nice because they are nice to eat and their flavour is lovely.

Cathan Eames (9)
Oakridge Junior School

All About Me

What happened to the dummy I sucked when I was 18 months old?
My dog ate it.
What happened to my first nappy when I was one?
Thrown away.
What happened to my clothes when I was two?
Went mouldy.
What happened to my doll when I was three?
I lost it at playschool.
What happened to my shoes when I was four?
Sold them.
What happened to my first football when I was five?
It burst.
What happened to my slide when I was six?
Broke.
What happened to my football cards when I was seven?
Swapped them.
What happened to my purse when I was eight?
Vanished.
What happened to my football boots when I was nine?
Got too small.
Nothing left,
Nothing left,
Will I have to buy it all again for my children?

Hannah Allmark & Cerys Cousins (9)
Portway Junior School

Questions And Answers

Where's my toy that I played with at one?
Gone forever.
Where's my bottle that I had when I was two?
Thrown away.
Where's the teddy tortoise that I had when I was three?
Mouldy.
Where's the blanket that made me go to sleep at four?
Lost.
Where's the house that I played with at five?
Fallen down.
Where's the doll that I slept with at six?
Gone.
Where's the toy monkey that I had at seven?
Nowhere to be seen.
Where's the blanket with spots that I had at eight?
Blown away.
Where's my favourite hair band that I had at nine?
Cut.
Where's it all gone?
I'm ten now and I have nothing.

Where has it gone?
All gone . . .
All gone . . .

Lauryn Newman (8)
Portway Junior School

Cheeky

Cheeky cheeks, always late!
That's a thing no one mistakes.
Never listen, never care,
Never buy my own underwear,
Swerving in and out the shops,
Mum I'm asking you to buy my socks.

Siân Allen (9) & Tayla Jade Moody (8)
Portway Junior School

Who Likes?

Who likes playing?
Me.
Who likes sleeping?
Me.
Who likes friends?
Me.
Who likes running?
Me.
Who likes TV?
Me.
Who likes Nintendo Wiis?
Me.
Who likes Nintendo DS's?
Me.
Who likes the world?
Me.
Who likes me?
Me.
Best of all I like cool people and hanging out with my friends!
But who likes hard work?
Not me!

Courtney Tobin (9)
Portway Junior School

I've Got . . .

I've got brown hair,
I've got blue eyes,
I've got pink lips to no surprise,
I've got small feet,
I've got small eyes,
I've got small fingers but I'm wise,
I've got a nice mum,
I've got a nice dad,
I've got a nice brother and I'm glad,
So look at all the things I've got,
Will you get there? I hope not!

Abigail Jones (9)
Portway Junior School

About Me

My name is Kayleigh,
I am eight years old,
My brother's name is Daniel Lee,
The top of my dad's head is bald,
I was born in 1999,
I was born in England,
I have a skinny spine,
I'd love to be in a rock band,
I have very long hair,
Alice, my sister, has short but fair
'Course I like my parties,
Things that I just can't bear,
I really don't like peas,
But I'm sure I like my sweets,
As well as my chocolate,
But not as much as
I love my mum and dad.

Kayleigh Morris (8)
Portway Junior School

Who Likes?

Who likes rabbits?
Who likes cats?
Who likes puppies
That sit on mats?

Who likes swimming?
Who likes sport?
Who likes winning
On a Saturday course?

Who likes art?
Who likes smart?
Who likes cars driving,
Round the school?

Cara-Leigh Bishop & Gemma Bennett (9)
Portway Junior School

You Can't Buy Friendship

Friendship is a special thing,
Not everyone can buy it,
Even if your daddy says,
'Come on let's try it!'

Then you buy them ice cream,
And things galore,
You still can't buy your friendship,
Not even like before.

A friend is real,
A friend is kind,
A friend will not have money on their mind.

My friends are friends,
Who will be there till the end.

Mikela Donnelly (9)
Portway Junior School

Who Likes Pets . . .

Who likes rabbits?

I do!

Who likes kittens?

I do!

Who likes dogs?

I do!

Who likes pets?

I like everything!

Charlene Dible (9)
Portway Junior School

Best Friends

Best friends . . .
Always stick together,
Whatever the weather.

Best friends . . .
Help us out,
Without a doubt.

Running here,
Running there,
Best friends run everywhere!

Best friends . . .
Care and share,
Always laugh,
If they break a chair.

Best friend . . .
Sometimes fight,
Even though they,
Stop at night.

Running here,
Running there,
Best friends run everywhere!

Best friends,
Like to eat,
Something very, very sweet,
Best friends.

Chloe Brookes (8) & Lizzie White (9)
Portway Junior School

Who Likes?

Who likes kisses?
Me.
Who likes Portway School?
Me.
Who likes hugs?
Me.
Who likes maths?
Me.
Who likes getting spoilt by your mother?
Me.
Who likes literacy?
Me.
Who likes sisters?
Me.
Who likes art?
Me.
But best of all I like my mum,
Tucking me into bed.

Dana Shelley (9)
Portway Junior School

Me

Who likes hugs?
Me.
Who likes cheese?
Me.
Who likes going on the DS?
Me.
Who likes drumming?
Me.

But best of all,
I like my friends, my friends,
Without them I'd be nothing.

Liam Russell (9)
Portway Junior School

Who Likes?

Who likes candy?
Me.

Who likes chocolate?
Me.

Who likes sweets?
Me.

Who likes caramel chocolate?
Me.

Who likes toffee?
Me.

Who likes fudge?
Me.

But most of all I like Portway School with the
School subjects because my school is such fun.

Jing-Ying Wong (9)
Portway Junior School

Who Likes?

Who likes football?
Me.
Who likes TV?
Me.
Who likes Star Wars?
Me.
Who likes Transformers?
Me.
Who likes cats?
Me.
Who likes dogs?
Me.
But when I get put in bed
And I get tucked up, I get a kiss.

Ronan White (9)
Portway Junior School

What Do You Like?

Football?
What!
Aero dynamics?
How?
Dancing,
Eh!
Wrestling?
Nah!
Table tennis?
Can you hit the ball?
What do you like?
I don't know.
Rally?
Prefer races,
Olympics?
Winter ones?
I give in,
What do you like?
Family and friends.

Alex Morling (9)
Portway Junior School

Who Likes This? Me!

Who likes skateboarding?
Me.
Who likes hockey?
Me.
Who likes TV?
Me.
Who likes going on the Wii, PS2 and a DS?
Me.
Who likes tidying their room?
Not me!

Harvey Sullivan (9)
Portway Junior School

Me

Who likes cuddles?
Me.
Who likes pizza?
Me.
Who likes TV?
Me.
Who likes PS3?
Who likes DS?
Me.
Who likes Spain?
Me.
Who likes Wii?
Me.
But best of all I like my family
Because they look after me all the time.

Matthew Corbett (8)
Portway Junior School

Who Likes Hugs?

Who likes hide-and-seek?
Me.
Who likes playing it?
Me.
Who likes going for a walk?
Me.
Who likes bedtime?
Me.
Who likes books?
Me.
Who likes Portway School?
Me.
But most of all
I like riding on my bike,
Round and round and round.

Cassie Clementine Shearer (8)
Portway Junior School

Who Likes Dogs?

Who likes dogs?
Me.
Who likes films?
Me.
Who likes pizza?
Me.
Who likes Wiis?
Me.
Who likes hugs?
Me.
Who likes sport?
Me.
But best of all
I like my family.

Stanley North (8)
Portway Junior School

Who Likes?

Who likes sweets?
Me.
Who likes gym?
Me.
Who likes friends?
Me.
Who likes family?
Me.
Who likes chocolate?
Me.
Who likes shiny things?
Me.
But most of all I like hanging out
With my family and friends.

Hannah Sullivan (8)
Portway Junior School

Who Likes . . .

Who likes rabbits?
Me.
Who likes cuddles?
Me.
Who likes tickles?
Me.
Who likes sweets?
Me.
Who likes squeezes?
Me.
Who likes their mum and dad?
Me.
Who likes their family?
Me.
Who likes golf?
Me.
But best of all,
I like my family because they
Feed me and care for me.

Hannah Wood (9)
Portway Junior School

Me

Who likes Mum?
Me.
Who likes Dad?
Me.
Who likes cars?
Me.
Who likes Doctor Who?
Me.
But best of all, I like my family
Because they look after me
And give me my favourite things.

Hayden Coyne (8)
Portway Junior School

Who Likes?

Who likes football?
Me.
Who likes Mum?
Me.
Who likes Dad?
Me.
Who likes toys?
Me.
Who likes TV?
Me.
Who likes PSP?
Me.
But most of all,
I like my friend.

Jordan Day (9)
Portway Junior School

Missing Things

Who stole the earrings?
Me.
Who stole the necklace?
Me.
Who stole the bracelet?
Me.
Who stole the dress?
Me.
Who stole the shoes?
Me.

I am so naughty . . . so naughty!
I love shiny things to collect because . . .
I'm a magpie!

Amber Casselton (9)
Portway Junior School

Untitled

Who likes football?
Me.
Who likes England?
Me.
Who likes chocolate?
Me.
Who likes Jordan, the country?
Me.
Who likes swimming?
Me.
Who likes holidays?
Me.
Who likes basketball?
Me.
Who likes family?
Me.
Who likes school?
Not me!

Moath Alshryfat (9)
Portway Junior School

Who Likes?

Who likes TV?
Me.
Who likes Doctor Who?
Me.
Who likes dogs?
Me.
Who likes computers?
Me.
But most of all I like my family,
Because they look after me.

Luke Holden (8)
Portway Junior School

Me

Who likes chocolate?
Me.
Who likes PSP?
Me.
Who likes Man United?
Me.
Who likes TV?
Me.
Who likes Christmas?
Me.
Who likes J20?
Me.
But most of all I like to play football,
With my best friend Kieran because
We can be really good at playing together.

Charlie Rogers (8)
Portway Junior School

Where Is My Old Stuff?

Where is the blanket from when I was one month old?
In the bin,
Where are all the teddies from when I was one?
Lost somewhere,
Where are all the clothes I had when I was two?
In the loft,
Where are all the toys I loved when I was three?
Sold to people,
Where's the bed I slept in when I was four?
Your sister sleeps on it,
Where are all my things?
Why are they all gone?

Kerry Louise Allen & Jessica-Leigh Nixon (9)
Portway Junior School

Who Likes That?

Who likes cars?
Me.
Who likes food?
Me.
Who likes friends?
Me.
Who likes PS3?
Me.
Who likes chocolate?
Me.
Who likes TV?
Me.
Who likes the world?
Me.
Who likes sleeping?
Me.
But most of all,
I like jacket potatoes,
Beans and cheese!
Lovely!
Who likes school?
Not me!

Declan Hughes (9)
Portway Junior School

When I Went Fishing

When I went fishing,
I caught a great big pike,
Then I dropped it and
It swam away,
I went back the next day,
I never caught a pike again,
When I went fishing,
When I went fishing.

Alex Roberts (9) & Jenny Upton (8)
Portway Junior School

Ben

My name is Ben,
I am a cat,
I sometimes think I am the moon or wood,
Also I sometimes think I am Ben the superman,
One day I fell out of a flat and landed on a mat,
One day I thought I was a raven, on the theme park waves.

Gregor Corcoran (8)
Portway Junior School

The Magic Box
(Based on 'Magic Box' by Kit Wright)

I will put in my box . . .

The sight of animals running wildly,
The touch of a lion's mane
Warm from the sun,
And the smell of a newborn
Animal known only by its mum.

I will put in my box . . .

The sound of a small bright bird tweeting
As the trees sway,
A feel of a tiny, quiet, chocolate coloured mouse
Making its way to its home,
And also the sight of a black cat
Sat on the edge of the old cobweb covered wall.

I will put in my box . . .

A shine of the moon as the stars twinkled,
A bright smile from a baby girl,
And finally a magical wish from everyone in the world.

Abby Arnold (11)
Stoke Park Junior School

All About Me

I live in an old basement where
I live alone and only alone,
I can smell the revolting burnt food
That lingers in the corners of me,
I have been tossed around to
Cook for the queen,
I am a thousand burns old.
I remember being a home for mice.
I am afraid of being burnt
Down and never to be used again.
I wish to be used to cook
Fantastic food and not for mice to live in me.
I once overhead that my owners were moving home
And that no one would come and buy this house.
I don't understand why I got left alone,
I will never know.
I just want to have an owner who will cook on me,
My name is Scullery.

Aleesha Head (10)
Stoke Park Junior School

The Magic Box
(Based on 'Magic Box' by Kit Wright)

I will put in my box . . .
A massive mountain from the rusty desert,
The sound of a born baby crying for help,
A toy shark from the mighty ocean.

I will put in my box . . .
A forgotten key from an ancient jail,
A dinosaur's foot which has been bitten off,
A ten-gallon hat from a pint-sized cowboy.

My box is created from steel, gold and silver,
With metal corners and a hand as a handle,
Its hinges are a heartbeat.

Lewis Dawkins (10)
Stoke Park Junior School

The Magic Box
(Based on 'Magic Box' by Kit Wright)

I will put in my box . . .
The voice of the wailing wind
The glow of the moon on a dark, winter night,
And the ashes of a burnt down house from many years ago.

I will put in my box . . .
The heat from the sun on a warm summer's day,
A torn shoe from a Victorian boy,
And a teaspoon of dust from a dilapidated house.

I will put in my box . . .
The footsteps of an elderly dog,
The crash of a wave hitting another,
And a spoonful of a grey cloud.

My box is created from crystal
And snow and the skin of a snake,
With a slice of a rainbow and the scales of a dragon,
It's hinges are the toe joints of prehistoric birds.

Jed Ponsford (10)
Stoke Park Junior School

The Magic Box
(Based on 'Magic Box' by Kit Wright)

I will put in my box . . .
A beam of a moon caught at midnight,
Fire from a bonfire that is as bright as the sun,
The blast from a rocket ship as it speeds into space.

I will put in my box . . .

A rusty key that opens a gate to a castle in China,
A Pacific Ocean wave crashing onto a desert island shore,
The bedtime kisses from a loving mum.

My box is created from stone, silver and lava,
With bronze sunrays and secrets within,
Its hinges are the knuckle joins of a cavemen.

Charley Snow (11)
Stoke Park Junior School

The Magic Box
(Based on 'Magic Box' by Kit Wright)

I will put in my box . . .
A creak of an ancient door,
The slimiest, shiniest, slipiest slug,
The roar of the rushing sea.

I will put in my box . . .
A shattered letter from Roman times,
A sparkly sun setting in the west,
A cowboy horse's hoof from the Wild West.

I will put in my box . . .
A dog's bark when they're in danger,
The crackle of pebbles being washed upon the shore,
A silver segment of hair.

My box is designed with . . .
Rubies and emeralds,
With a rainbow arched and fairies on top,
Its hinges are the jaws of crocodiles caught
In the depths of the Amazon.

Gemma Bevis-Lacey (10)
Stoke Park Junior School

Tales Of A Peak

I love the view of a string of other friends,
But the feel of the brush of snow on my top,
Makes me feel cold inside,
I've witnessed Earth being created,
Now I'm seeing it destroyed,
I've existed longer than your species has ever walked,
I recall the time when parts of me were falling off,
I have nightmares of hurting people using my strength,
My dreams include living forever,
I've been told I'm monumental and massive,
But I want to know, why am I an attraction?
I am a mountain.

Ben Haynes (10)
Stoke Park Junior School

Untitled

I live in a cottage surrounded by a forest of trees,
This cottage is small and squared,
In a dusty sitting room, that's where I am,
I'm touched by the fingers of two people
Who have lived here for many years,
When the old lady and man tuck themselves into bed and sleep,
I become awake,
I moved out of my old house but I've here for countless years
And lived in many homes.
I remember being bought by these two humans and
Feeling glad and safe,
I was afraid that they would destroy me and throw me away.
I wish to be polished and well cleaned,
Because I feel stained and would like to be dirt free.
The man was speaking to the lady quietly,
I listened, they were thinking about getting rid of me,
I mean I keep them warm,
But they hardly ever put me on.

I am a fireplace.

Ashlee Moore
Stoke Park Junior School

If You Want To See A Dolphin . . .

If you want to see a dolphin,
You must go down to the shiny, deep blue sea,
I know a dolphin who's living down there,
She's a jumper, she's kind,
Yes if you really want to see a dolphin,
You must go down the shiny, deep blue sea,
'Dolphin come out,
Dolphin come out,
Dolphin come out,'
And she will come out,
But don't go away,
She is kind.

Sophie Townsend (8)
Stoke Park Junior School

Do You Know Who I Am?

I live in a dusty old classroom full of children,
I can feel their rough fingers brushing past me,
I can hear them getting on with their work
And playing with their friends.
I get upset when they don't treat me the way they should,
Ripping pages and breaking my spine.
I was made in the days when the teachers were strict,
And they treated me with care.
I remember being stacked in a tiny box with others of my type,
I am afraid of being torn beyond repair,
I dream of being alone and being treated with proper care.
I once heard that I was no use and that
I might as well be thrown away,
I do not understand that I am no use,
My name is 'Dictionary!'

Abbie Carter (11)
Stoke Park Junior School

Big And Brave
(Based on 'Magic Box' by Kit Wright)

I will put in my box . . .
A dazzling mountain standing tall,
Hills of green covered by wildlife,
And a stormy cloud, loud and gloomy.

I will put in my box . . .
A dark black insect,
A giant mole hole,
And the wing of a Spitfire,
Shot down in its finest hour.

My box is hand crafted from iron,
That sparkles when light hits it,
With nails on top that grant a wish,
And a black key that keeps it shut tight.

Christopher Hopkins (10)
Stoke Park Junior School

The Magic Box
(Based on 'Magic Box' by Kit Wright)

I will put in my box . . .
An orange and pink sun,
Setting where the rainbow ends,
The pinch of the claws from a crab
Catching its prey,
The first chuckle of a cheerful baby.

I will put in my box . . .
The scent of a rich melted chocolate
Running down the edge of a cake,
The sound of wailing wolves on top of a mountain,
The stroke of pebbles crashing down a waterfall.

My box is created from seaweed so shiny
It will hurt your eyes,
With diamonds in every corner and stars on every edge,
Its hinges are raindrops collected from flowers in a winter meadow.

Isobel Hardy (10)
Stoke Park Junior School

If You Want To See A Meerkat . . .
(Based on the poem 'Alligator' by Grace Nichols)

If you want to see a Meerkat,
You must go to the hot, sandy Kalahari desert.

I know a Meerkat
Who's living down there,
He's a-sharp, he's a-quick,
He's not afraid of us.

Yes, if you really want to see a Meerkat,
You must quietly go to the Kalahari desert,
Go down the dusty, Kalahari desert and say,
'Meerkat mama Meerkat mama,
Meerkat, mamaaaa!'

And she will rise,
But don't stay - *go home.*

Isaac Porter (8)
Stoke Park Junior School

If You Want To See A Penguin . . .
(Based on the poem 'Alligator' by Grace Nichols)

If you want to see a penguin,
You must go down to freezing Antarctica,
And wrap up warm,
I know a penguin who's living down there,
He's a-big, he's a-biter, he's a-snipper,
Yes, if you really want to see a penguin,
You must go down to freezing Antarctica,
And wrap up warm,
Go down carefully and say,
'Emperor penguin,
Emperor penguin,
Emperor penguinnnnnn!'
And he will jump up from the cold water,
But don't stay there -
Run for your life!

Bethany Vokes (8)
Stoke Park Junior School

If You Want To See A Dolphin . . .
(Based on the poem 'Alligator' by Grace Nichols)

If you want to see a dolphin,
You must go to the lovely beautiful blue sea,
I know a quiet, small dolphin who's living down there,
He's a-quiet, he's a-grey, he's a-small, he's a-squirt water!
Yes if you really want to see a dolphin,
You must go to the lovely beautiful blue sea,
Go down to the gentle waved sea and say,
'Lovely dolphin,
Lovely dolphin,
Lovely dolppppphin!'
And go down to see a dolphin,
But remember to
Stroke him!

Kierney Frampton (7)
Stoke Park Junior School

If You Want To See A Penguin . . .
(Based on the poem 'Alligator' by Grace Nichols)

You must go to the icy, cold, Southern Hemisphere,
Where they live.

I know a penguin
Who's living down there,
He's a feisty, pecking machine,
He's a devil, when it comes to fighting.

Yes, if you really want to see a penguin,
You must go to the icy, cold, Southern Hemisphere,
Where they live.

Go down the shiny, ocean land,
And say,
'Penguin,
Penguin,
Penguinnnn!'

And don't stick around,
Because he'll eat you up for breakfast!

Daniel Brierley (8)
Stoke Park Junior School

If You Want To See A Dolphin . . .
(Based on the poem 'Alligator' by Grace Nichols)

If you want to see a dolphin,
You must go to the bottom of the deep, deep blue sea,
I know a dolphin who's living down there,
He's a-lovely, he's a-cute, he's a-harmless,
Yes if you really want to see a dolphin,
You must go to the bottom of the deep, deep blue sea,
Go to the bottom of the deep, deep blue sea and say,
'Come to me dolphin!
Come to me dolphin!
Come to me dolphin!'
And he will appear in front of your eyes,
But don't run away, stay and play.

Elena Beckett-Oxenham (7)
Stoke Park Junior School

If You Want To See A Tiger . . .
(Based on the poem 'Alligator' by Grace Nichols)

If you want to see a tiger,
You must go down to the hot, sticky jungle,
With enormous plants and trees,
I know a tiger
Who's living down there,
He's a-fierce, he's a-scary,
He's a-large, he's a-killer,
Yes, if you really want to see a tiger,
You must go down to the hot, sticky jungle,
With enormous plants and trees,
Go down very quietly and say,
'Tiger dadda,
Tiger dadda,
Tiger daddaaa!'
And he'll open his eyes,
But don't hang about,
Run as fast as you can!

Kyle Patel (8)
Stoke Park Junior School

Freedom

You are free to do what you want,
You are powerful.
Never stop dreaming because dreams might come true.
Freedom is joyful and happy,
You should always be happy and safe,
You don't have to be happy to be free,
You can be sad to be free.
No one should tell you what to do,
It's good to say no!
You dream about being what you want,
You think about having something that you want,
You are free to do what you want, when you want,
This is what freedom means.

Georgia Hall (10)
Stoke Park Junior School

Dreaming

When I am sad,
I think of love,
Which always
Cheers me up,
Am I thinking of freedom?

Then I think of
All of the feelings
That I've kept inside,
Am I thinking of freedom?

I think of rabbits,
I think of cats,
Every animal
I can,
Am I thinking of freedom?

Then I picture
Five bunnies
Playing together,
Happy as can be,
Am I thinking of freedom?

Two older bunnies
Come along and
Call the youngest one in,
Am I thinking of freedom?

The youngest one was me
And the older ones are my parents,
They take me home and tuck me into bed,
Am I thinking of freedom?

My parents kiss me on the cheek
And wander out the room,
I open my eyes and there they are,
I had been in a whole dream,
Am I thinking of freedom?

Yes dreaming is a part of being free!

Lauren Foster (10)
Stoke Park Junior School

Rain Poem

I am playful to a fault,
When I puddle in the street,
I provide a stomping ground,
For kids with happy feet,
I bring them lots of laughter,
With wet and muddy stains,
They take me home with them,
But wash me down the drain.

The thunder is violent,
The lightning is incredible,
The rain falls down on me,
I run, it follows me,
My hair gets wet and turns curly,
Oh how I hate the rain,
I hide in my room but it traps me,
Doom and gloom!

Rachel Thompson (11)
Stoke Park Junior School

If You Want To See A Fox . . .
(Based on the poem 'Alligator' by Grace Nichols)

If you want to see a fox,
You must go to the dark, scary forest,
I know a fox
Who's living down there,
He's a-mean, he's a-big, he's a-fierce,
He's a-growler,
Yes, if you really want to see a fox,
You must go down to the dark forest,
Go down and say,
'Fox, fox, come to me,
I want to eat you for my tea'.
And he'll come up to you,
But do not say 'Good boy!'

Run for it!

Olivia Norman (7)
Stoke Park Junior School

If You See A Tiger . . .
(Based on the poem 'Alligator' by Grace Nichols)

If you want to see a tiger,
You must go down to the smelly, green, fresh,
And hot jungle,
I know a tiger
Who's living down there,
He's a-fast, he's a-hunter, he's a-scary,
He's a-roamer,
Yes, if you really want to see a tiger,
You must go down to the smelly, green, fresh,
And hot jungle,
Go down quietly to that jungle and say,
'Tiger daddy,
Tiger daddy,
Tiger daddyyyyy!'
And he'll pounce,
But don't stay too long,
Run for your life!

Ben Bramall, Joshua Hughes, Simon Hancock, Harley White, Adam Wastney (7), Ciarán Cooper & Aidan Asquith (8)
Stoke Park Junior School

Freedom

Freedom is very special to people
Because it is not that often they have it.
I am free to explore, free to move,
Free to think, smell and rest,
Freedom is to have personal space and privacy,
Freedom on your own away from your friends and noise,
Freedom brings love to all to share and happiness everywhere,
Confined in a space, locked away in a desk,
Freedom is open skies and sunny places.

Daniel Hibberd (9)
Stoke Park Junior School

Freedom

It is the summer holidays,
No homework, no learning,
I'm free for six weeks,
No rules, no rules.
I'm on top of the world,
I can say what I want,
Not in school, hooray!
No rules, no rules.
I feel like I'm flying free,
No slavery, it's freedom,
You don't have to do what people say,
No rules, no rules.
You're free to do what you want,
You dream about being on top of the world,
Nobody should bother you,
No rules, no rules.

Keiran Murray (9)
Stoke Park Junior School

Freedom Poetry

Freedom . . . having fun and being able
To do what you want, when you want,
Is this what freedom means?

To have time to think
And time alone to gaze at the hot, burning sun,
Is this what freedom means?

To look up to shining stars,
And to see them twinkling like the
Pretty moon in the sky,
Is this what freedom means?

Freedom is having space to think
And be yourself and being happy with yourself,
This is what freedom means!

Georgia Blake (9)
Stoke Park Junior School

Freedom

It's the summer holidays,
No school for six weeks,
I'm free, I'm free,
No rules, no lessons, no teachers,
No waking up early,
I'm free, I'm free.
Imaginations go wild,
No one can control me,
I'm free, I'm free.
I'm on top of the world,
Free to do whatever I like,
I'm free, I'm free.
I don't have to answer to anyone.

I'm free to talk when I like,
Free to express myself,
I'm free, I'm free,
I feel invincible.
I'm . . .
Overjoyed,
Have butterflies in my tummy,
I can play when I like,
I'm free, I'm free.
To me that's what freedom means.

Chloe Jarvis (10)
Stoke Park Junior School

I Want Freedom

I want freedom, there will be enough money,
I want freedom, it'll feel as sweet as honey.

Freedom means no poverty,
Freedom is a soaring eagle,
Freedom talks of warm spring days,
Freedom is a flying butterfly.

I want freedom, to be sky high,
I want freedom, no one to defy.

Freedom means no rules at all,
Freedom is glossy, white silk,
Freedom tells of glowing angels,
Freedom is a snowy, white cloud.

I want freedom, to stand on a mountain,
I want freedom, to sing like a robin.

Freedom means no rich, no poor,
Freedom is a fair, kind world,
Freedom tells of lovely memories,
Freedom is a lovely day.

I want freedom, there'll be enough food,
I want freedom, it'll all be good.

Abi Carr (9)
Stoke Park Junior School

Freedom

To be free as a bee flying through the sky,
To have freedom of speech,
To do what we like when we like,
Is this what freedom is?

Freedom to say what we want, when we want,
Freedom not to be told what to do,
To be allowed to go where we like,
Is this what freedom is?

Freedom not to be slaves,
Freedom to make our own choices,
Freedom from not having to follow rules,
And freedom can lead to happiness.

Freedom is like being at the top of the world,
Freedom not to be bossed around,
Freedom to speak for yourself,
Is this what freedom is?

Jack Horn (10)
Stoke Park Junior School

Freedom

Freedom is an amazing thing,
It's like a never-ending open road,
And you choose the way to go.

Freedom is good, freedom is bad,
Freedom is happy, freedom is sad,
When you have freedom, you should feel glad.

Freedom is a hard thing to describe,
Like why there are spikes on a porcupine,
Freedom makes you feel happy and warm inside,
Like when a baby eagle is learning to fly.

Gregory Lay (10)
Stoke Park Junior School

Freedom

Freedom is peace,
Freedom is where you can sing and shout out loud to the open world,
Where there is freedom you can dance on the open roads,
Sit down and pick daisies calmly,
You can be free,
Be free from working,
Be free from being a slave,
Be free from being told what to do,
Be free from a hardworking life,
You can be free,
Climb the mountains,
Run down the hill,
Have a laugh with your mates,
Sit down on a hill,
You can be free.

You can glide like a bird,
That is freedom,
Run like a cheetah,
That is freedom,
You can be free!

Natasha Keith (9)
Stoke Park Junior School

A Colourful Day

I see the whole world,.
I can feel the fluffy clouds brush past my shiny arch,
I have a cold body,
I am centuries of years old,
I remember making people smile,
I'm afraid of fading away forever,
I dream of being in the sky every day,
I hear the wind rushing past me,
I don't understand why I'm so colourful,
My name is Rainbow!

Lauren Powell (10)
Stoke Park Junior School

The Magic Box
(Based on the poem 'Magic Box' by Kit Wright)

I will put in my box . . .
The square bowling ball that cries,
A weeping willow in the night,
A pure, red-hot sun.

I will put in my box . . .
A breeze from the coldest point of the North Pole,
A tree with a wooden heart,
A thunderbolt from a dark cloud tornado.

I will put in my box . . .
The hiss of a sea serpent,
The sound of an erupting volcano,
The sparklers of a magical rainbow.

I will put in my box . . .
A horn from the Minotaur,
A snake from Medusa,
A tentacle from the Kraken.

My box is fashioned from:
Emerald, ruby and sapphire,
With secret diamond corners,
And a hint of amber.

I shall surf in my box,
On the high rollers of the wild Antarctic,
Then land ashore on a beach with the
Colour of the sun.

Bradley Reeves (10)
Stoke Park Junior School

Freedom

No rules,
No restrictions,
No one controlling you,
Freedom?

Able to express yourself,
Can say what you want,
No teachers,
Freedom?

Are you free?
Need rules,
Need restrictions,
Need someone controlling you.

Not able to express yourself,
Not able to say what you want,
You have no teachers,
Freedom?

Rules; not too many,
Restrictions; not too many,
People controlling you; not too much.

Able to express yourself,
Say what you want most of the time,
Have teachers,
This is freedom!

James Ross (10)
Stoke Park Junior School

Freedom

Freedom is valuable,
It treats us fair,
From wide, open space,
To lovely fresh air.

Free from jail,
Free from war,
Being controlled will be no more.

There is freedom all around us,
There's lots and lots and lots,
Not every one of us has freedom,
But for us it never stops.

If you stand out in the garden,
Thinking about wars,
Don't think about getting caught in one,
Because freedom is all yours!

James Dilworth (10)
Stoke Park Junior School

What Am I?

I can see tiny ants scampering around,
I feel tall and mighty in the sun,
Centuries have passed my eyes,
I can taste the bristling cold air at my peak,
I am afraid of my sides crumbling down,
I dream of never having to stand alone.

I am a mountain.

Ashleigh Curl (10)
Stoke Park Junior School

Freedom

Freedom is my special day,
No school, no rules, all time to play,
Sunshine shining in a glare,
Do a flip up in the air.

Free to move, free to stare,
Free to say how much you care,
Free to jump, free to run, free to have lots of fun.

Space to be alone you see,
So much fun, fun it has to be,
Free to say what you think,
A light will shine with everything.

Freedom is my holiday,
No one to stop me on my way,
I've never felt like this today,
Now I've got time to come and pray.

Harriet Johnson (10)
Stoke Park Junior School

What Am I?

I can see life passing by,
I feel alone every year,
I have bends going around the world,
I am free to flow anywhere,
I remember the first light upon these lands,
I am afraid that my path will be blocked,
I dream of being crystal clear,
I heard people building wooden beasts,
I do not understand why people pollute me,
My name is River.

Andrew Pritchard (11)
Stoke Park Junior School

Freedom

Is freedom a spirit,
Light watching down on people?

Or is it sitting down in the summer breeze,
Watching a bird gliding up high?

Are you dreaming to be a hero
Or to help round the world?

Not to be trapped in a house?

You're free to sing and play,
And you have the right to learn,
Or to play on a field,
Are you free?
Can you do what you want?

Are you as free as you want?
Can you go where you want?
If you are free, no hassle,
Is this what freedom means?

Bailey Moore (9)
Stoke Park Junior School

What Am I?

I can see people pointing and laughing,
I can taste fear,
I remember always being wanted,
I was at the top,
I am afraid of being recycled,
I dream of someone buying me,
I am a book.

Fraser McGowan (10)
Stoke Park Junior School

Freedom

Life is all round,
It's in my heart,
Apart,
It's full of joy, life,
Most of all honour.

It has the core of my heart
In its hand,
I know this may sound
Silly, but
I shall remember
In the light,
For all of all
My heart pumps,
My eyes water and
Fall down my cheek,
Freedom is in my grasp.

Summer Hammond (10)
Stoke Park Junior School

Freedom

An endless stretch of road,
Only hope can guide you along it,
Freedom is something not everyone gets,
But most are lucky to get it.

I have freedom of choice,
Opinion, belief and speech,
I stand alone on top of a hill,
No one around me, I'm all alone,
That is freedom to me.

Max Copsey (9)
Stoke Park Junior School

Freedom

Through the night and day,
I stick to my religion,
I watch, I pray,
I have a free choice of religion.

Through the night and day
I speak aloud,
I talk a lot, I might say
I have the freedom of speech.

Through the night and day,
I save myself some space,
I always have space when I lay,
I have the freedom of space.

When you're free, you find out,
Once in a while you have to be alone from home,
Where night falls and day breaks,
Our spirits are set free!

Holly Mumford (10)
Stoke Park Junior School

Freedom

I drift away like a balloon caught in the wind,
The troubles of life can not bother me here,
500 metres above the ground.
In a pair of binoculars as I see my house,
It was still pretty small even in the binoculars,
But it still made me smile,
Now I am completely free.
I shall leave this foul place and never come back,
Now all I need is a destination,
I thought Ireland or maybe Wales,
I turned the right way, then I set off away,
Say hello to a new life and a new beginning.

Luke Baker (9)
Stoke Park Junior School

Freedom

Freedom is special,
Freedom to me is in my heart,
No school, no rules, no timetable to start,
I go on holiday,
I have fresh air,
I'm free from people,
I have no fear,
Free to move,
Free to care,
Freedom is running through the air,
Freedom to say what I think.

Without freedom life would be glum,
No space to move,
No new places to see,
Scared to speak what's in my heart,
It's sad if you have no freedom in your heart,
Freedom - keep it safe every day.

Jenna Anderson (9)
Stoke Park Junior School

Freedom

Freedom is something you can do on your own,
You're king of the world.

Freedom is to have no school, no homework,
And no rules, you can do what you want.

Freedom is to play around outside and
Playing with your friends.

Going down to the shop and having no one
There to spoil your fun.

Have open spaces, no traffic to stop you going.

You can speak whenever you want.

Freedom is free, it's laughter and the road never ends.

Charlie Andrews (10)
Stoke Park Junior School

Freedom

As free as a bird,
When you are soaring,
Flying, gliding through a gentle breeze,
Is this what freedom means?

When you can dream what you want,
Maybe being a doctor, pilot or maybe even a police officer,
Is this what freedom means?

When you are allowed to say what you feel,
Express your opinion, no matter what other people think,
Is this what freedom means?

Is freedom when you are allowed to do what you want,
With nobody to stop you,
Is this what freedom means?

When you are allowed to be alone,
Have some peace and quiet,
A little time on your own,
Is this what freedom means?

Jim Dawkins (9)
Stoke Park Junior School

What Am I?

I live at school, my neck is long,
Sometimes I hear voices,
I have a bulb that lights up words and pictures,
I've sat at the front of the classroom for ages,
I remember being fed a light bulb for the first time,
I'm afraid of blowing up!
I dream of being more hi-tech as I'm not used very often,
I've heard people talking about getting a newer and better model,
I don't understand why I just sit in the corner.

My name is Overhead Projector.

Jack Bailey (11)
Stoke Park Junior School

Freedom

Freedom is choice
To say what you want,
Do what you want,
What could be a better way?

Free from jail,
Free from war,
Free from the traffic jam,
But keep fresh air,
I'm free in the air,
You can do anything,
But keep it safe.

When you're high
In the sky,
You're king of the world.

Freedom . . .
Are you free?

James Wheable (10)
Stoke Park Junior School

What Am I?

I live on a wall where I can see trees and animals,
I can hear children playing games outside.
I have a tiny unnoticeable crack.
I'm too old to remember much,
But I do remember being cut.
I'm afraid of being smashed!
I wish I could be cleaned.
I overhear children's secrets,
I do not understand why they cover me with material.

My name is Window.

Summah Walker (10)
Stoke Park Junior School

Is That What Freedom Means?

As free as a soaring eagle,
When you are flying and gliding calmly
Up to the glinting stars,
Is this being free?

As free as floating dreams
In the light blue sky,
You dream of being
A pilot, an astronaut,
A doctor or a teacher,
Is this what freedom means?

Is freedom when you are allowed to do what you want?
And say what you want?
Is this being free?

Driving down a never-ending alleyway with no one around,
Driving round in a big 4X4 down a never-ending,
Dry, dusty road, alone . . .
Is this what freedom means?

Andrew Wood (10)
Stoke Park Junior School

What Am I?

I see a clean, tidy room from where I stand,
I can smell different perfumes combined together,
To make a bedroom lovely,
I love playing music, it is my favourite hobby.
I am brand new, just home from the boring shop.
I remember when I was wrapped up in smelly,
                             pretty paper for Christmas,
Then my owner set me free.
I'm afraid of getting dropped like my other friend.
I wish for more food, round like pizzas,
I wish my owner would play me, instead of watching TV,
I don't understand why I'm not played every day.

I am a CD player.

Tammy Dunford (11)
Stoke Park Junior School

Is This Your Freedom?

Do you have enough freedom?
Are you free from stress and annoyance,
Or are you trapped like a dog in a cage?
Are you as free as a bird,
As it soars through the wind?
Is this your freedom?

You can do as you like,
Stand up for your rights,
And say what you want to say,
When you want to say it,
Is this your freedom?

Do you have these things?
Are you able to stand up for your rights?
Do you want to live your life like a bird,
Flying through the sky?
Is this your freedom?

Can you do what you like?
Climb a mountain or relax in bed,
Stand under the sun and lie down?
Is this your freedom?

Are you able to feel safe?
If you fall, is there someone there to catch you?
Can you stand on a mountain and
Feel the wind in your face?
Is this your freedom?

Can you feel the wind in your face
And the breeze in your hair?
Are you free from crime and safe from robbers?
Is this your freedom?

Heather Thomson (10)
Stoke Park Junior School

Freedom

Are you innocent?
Why are you locked up?
Are you as free as a bird?
Why are you locked up?

Are you thankful for the world?
Why are you complaining?
Are you peaceful in your life?
Why are you complaining?

Are you on an open road?
Why are you stuck in traffic?
Are you in a peaceful land?
Why are you stuck in traffic?

Are you being cooled by the gentle breeze?
Why are you pushed back by the wind?
Are you being tanned by the warm sun?
Why are you being pushed back by the wind?

Anne Pritchard (9)
Stoke Park Junior School

Freedom Poem

Free as a bird, flying high,
Free as the wind in the sky,
Free of word, saying as like,
Free as everything, just like a kite.

Freedom is what you like,
Freedom is free from fight,
Freedom is no one to order,
Freedom is no one to forger.

Liberty is when you're free
Liberty is when you don't have to flee,
Liberty is when people don't attack.

Leila Harding (10)
Stoke Park Junior School

My Magic Box
(Based on the poem 'Magic Box' by Kit Wright)

I will put in my box . . .
The fur from a ferocious dog, tearing its toys apart,
The spots from a cheetah, in the bright sunlight,
And the whiff from stinky Bisto that has been left to rot.

I will put in my box . . .
The flash from the lightning storm,
Sharp against the treetops,
The mud from a horse shoe,
Galloping through the moonlight,
And the silky scales of a snake shedding its skin.

I will put in my box . . .
The ancient memories from that someone
Who left you behind,
The deep mysterious footprint,
Imprinted into the snow,
And the point from a shark's tooth,
Scratching and spiking the sea.

My box is fashioned with shooting stars,
With Neptune and Mars stuck to the top,
Meteors fly in and out of the corners,
And the hinges are made out of ruby coloured sparks.

I will leap into my box,
Jump deeper every time,
Making sure everything is there,
And I will stay there forever and ever,
Never to leap out again.

Ellen Cosgrove (10)
Stoke Park Junior School

Freedom

Freedom is the whirling wind of fresh air,
Freedom is joy,
Freedom is being cared for,
Freedom is having no limitations.

Freedom is being happy and excited,
Freedom is having presents,
Freedom is doing what you want,
Freedom is playing with who you like.

Freedom is being thankful for everything
You have been given,
Freedom is peace,
Freedom is being on a never-ending road,
Freedom is independence.

Freedom is lying in the hot, dazzling sun,
Freedom is a cold, crisp morning in the middle of winter,
Freedom is having fun,
Freedom is being relaxed in the breeze.

Freedom is being in the open world
Freedom is play,
Freedom is life,
Freedom is being proud.

Freedom is finding your inner self,
Freedom is light,
Freedom is lying in on a Sunday morning,
Freedom is being innocent,
This is what freedom means!

Harry Salmon (9)
Stoke Park Junior School

The Magic Box
(Based on the poem 'Magic Box' by Kit Wright)

I will put in the box . . .
A dancing dress that dims in the dark,
Ice from the mouth of a Japanese snowman,
The tip of a toe touching a tiger.

I will put in the box . . .
A doll with a terrible headache,
A taste of a golden apple from the China wall,
A shock from a jelly fish.

I will put in the box . . .
Seven sorry words spoken by a snake,
The first laugh from a newborn baby,
The first sign of dinosaurs found by archaeologists.

I will put in the box . . .
The bride and groom,
The sky from the north,
A surfer on a black horse,
A cowboy on a surfboard.

My box is designed with a drip of the Irish Sea,
With plants on the lid,
Its handle is a shark's tooth.

I shall surf in my box
On the lava of a volcano,
Then land on the sea floor,
The colour of the night sky.

Dan Page (11)
Stoke Park Junior School

The Magic Box
(Based on the poem 'Magic Box' by Kit Wright)

I will put in the box . . .
A roaring, red room,
A nun swimming alongside dolphins,
And a diver reading a bible.

I will put in the box . . .
A mannequin with a cold,
A breath of the whitest wind,
From Mount Everest,
A sudden splash of water
From a sea serpent.

I will put into the box . . .
Fifteen soft, satin secrets,
The first chirp of a newly born chick,
The final wish of the last genie.

I will put into the box . . .
The eleventh commandment,
A green sky and a blade of blue grass,
And the eighth colour of the rainbow.

My box is fashioned from . . .
Rubies of fire, and silver, and iron,
With wolverine fur and snakeskin,
The lid is a tree from the dawn of time.

I shall dig in my box,
And find a T-Rex,
I will bring it back to life,
And keep it as my pet.

Martha Richmond (10)
Stoke Park Junior School

The Magic Box
(Based on the poem 'Magic Box' by Kit Wright)

I will put in the box . . .
A shining snowman suffering from eternal night,
A golden key to unlock new worlds,
A bloodthirsty dragon breathing electric sparks.

I will put in the box . . .
Darkest fire from the underworld,
A box-headed fish with shimmering scales,
Friendly, flying spirits awoken from their graves.

I will put in the box . . .
A galloping pony from the land of rainbows,
My tiny teeth taken by the tooth fairy,
Cold, black diamonds from the darkest, deepest mine.

My box is fashioned from
Red rubies and white feathers from an owl and black bones,
With glass on the lid and iron in the corners,
Its hinges are the jaws of a crocodile.

Daniel Lipscombe (10)
Stoke Park Junior School

The Sea

The sea rushes calmly over the gleaming pebbles,
And reflects like a thousand mirrors,
Its colour is a dark, sapphire blue that flashes in the sunlight.

Its waves can be as high as houses,
And toss ships about like toy boats,
The sea is an unforgiving thing that will claim a life without a care.

The stones roll around like marbles,
A crash of a cymbal when a wave strikes the rocks,
Its tide ebbs and flows like a million people dancing the beat.

The sea can be as rough as a roller coaster ride,
And as smooth as a drive in the car,
The sea rushes like the Christmas shoppers.

James Thomas (11)
Stoke Park Junior School

Thunder

It starts off soft and white,
Thin marshmallows floating with the wind,
Hundreds of birds dodging their pathways,
Aeroplanes flying through.

Legless sheep roam the heavens,
Now they are obvious like God's pillows,
The fresh air wafts through their velvety skin,
Whilst they draw pictures in the sky.

They become grey and moody,
Not wanting to move,
Now they are looking sad and bored,
Never spreading a smile across the land.

They get angry, roaring and blowing,
No longer grey, totally pitch-black,
Wetness dripping from the blackness,
Into a stream of darkness.

Mollie Young (10)
Stoke Park Junior School

The Magic Box
(Based on the poem 'Magic Box' by Kit Wright)

I will put in the box . . .
An ice man on fire surfing from doom,
The moon to light up the world in the gloom,
A golden apple full of love.

I will put in the box . . .
The smallest lizard in the world,
A shiny unicorn to fill the sky,
A mystical spirit full of the past.

I will put in the box . . .
Magic stars lighting up the sky,
A broomstick to make me fly,
A window as shiny as ever.

My box is fashioned from silver and sequins
And love with diamonds on the lid and stars in the corners,
Its hinges are like jaws of a dragon's mouth.

Timothy Arthur (10)
Stoke Park Junior School

The Magic Box
(Based on the poem 'Magic Box' by Kit Wright)

I will put in the box . . .
The skin of a snake shivering in the wind,
A volcanic rock from an erupting volcano,
A star that is falling through the sky.

I will put in the box . . .
A corner of the moon in the night's sky,
A tree with a wooden heart,
A rabbit with no teeth.

I will put in the box . . .
A thunderbolt from the American tornado,
A puff of air from the Atlantic Ocean,
A surfer on a white horse,
A jockey on a surfboard.

My box is fashioned with ice and blue steel,
With clouds on the lid and
The hinges are dinosaur's toe joints.

I shall surf in my box on the great
Atlantic waves, then wash ashore,
On a yellow beach,
The colour of the sun.

James Hunt (11)
Stoke Park Junior School

The Magic Box
(Based on the poem 'Magic Box' by Kit Wright)

I will put in the box . . .
The bark of a dog as loud as a horn,
The scream of a stray cat in pain,
The gallop of a horse winning a race.

I will put in the box . . .
The soul of a photo saying hello,
A secret as secret as that from a forbidden book,
The flame from a burning candle flickering.

I will put in the box . . .
The smoke from the house's cigarette,
The cry of a newborn baby,
The sweet smell of hot chocolate.

My box is fashioned from . . .
An ancient dinosaur egg,
With a velociraptor fossil on the lid,
And scratch marks in the corners.

I shall hide my box,
In a cave,
In the tallest volcano.

Alice Warne (10)
Stoke Park Junior School

The Magic Box
(Based on the poem 'Magic Box' by Kit Wright)

I will put in the box . . .
Gold pennies to keep them safe,
A rusty key to open secrets,
A wizard's wand only to be used for good spells.

I will put in the box . . .
Gleaming, silver stars to help people find love,
Fire from a dragon's breath,
A magic moment.

I will put in the box . . .
A happy dog who will be my friend forever,
A fluffy pillow to sleep on at night,
A book that can read itself.

My box is fashioned from rubber and bronze and fur,
With mirrors on the lid and glitter in the corners,
Its hinges are cat's claws.

I shall fly in my box,
To Australia to see my uncle,
Then stay with him for a couple of days,
And walk over Sydney Harbour Bridge.

Ian Bevan (10)
Stoke Park Junior School

The Magic Box
(Based on the poem 'Magic Box' by Kit Wright)

I will put in the box . . .
Silver, shining bubbles to capture pain and suffering,
A lid of gold water shining in the gloom to help a lonely soul,
Yellow wishes, darting and swishing.

I will put in the box . . .
An owl at night laying darkness over the land,
A tiny candle lighting the sky to chase the evil spirits away,
A heart shining bright in the shadows.

I will put in the box . . .
A rainbow covering the world with happiness,
An icy key to unlock anyone's secrets.

My box is fashioned from pearls and iron and copper,
With a moon on the lid and gloom in the corners,
Its hinges are made of silver.

I will fly in my box,
On a magic carpet,
Then land on a jungle island
Called Chickamolatza.

Daniel Kane (10)
Stoke Park Junior School

The Magic Box
(Based on the poem 'Magic Box' by Kit Wright)

I will put in the box . . .
The sigh of sorrow on a cold, dark night,
The sleeping shiver from the pitch-black sky,
The howl and bark from a tall, hungry shadow.

I will put in the box . . .
The chuckle of a giggling baby,
Enclosed from the outside world,
A diary of a secret life from long, long a go,
A warm and cosy palace that stands tall,
And stately in the mountains.

I will put in the box . . .
The soft, smooth sand from a small, deserted beach,
The dazzling darkness dream from the night's sky,
A precious wish that stays with you forever.

My box is fashioned from glitter and rubies and tinsel,
With swirls on the lid and hearts in the corners,
Its hinges are stars, taken from the sky.

I shall fly in my box,
Soaring over the peaceful seas,
Then gliding till I find the land,
Where I can fulfil my dream.

Lauren Atkins (10)
Stoke Park Junior School

The Magic Box
(Based on the poem 'Magic Box' by Kit Wright)

I will put in the box . . .
A golden horse leaping across seasons,
Stars gleaming in the night sky,
A scale from a fire-breathing dragon.

I will put in the box . . .
A Chinese dragon speaking to clouds full of love,
A soul hurt and damaged by the suffering of people,
A knight's sword, restless and brave.

I will put in the box . . .
A turquoise night with a fresh, Atlantic breeze,
An angel with no love or beauty,
Ice fire from a snowman's nostrils.

My box is fashioned from the scales of a silver fish
And feathers from an eagle,
With steel stars on the lid and Christmas love in the corners,
Its hinges are made from a unicorn's Golden Horn.

I shall ride the high sky in my box,
Or a black bat, gliding swiftly,
Then I shall land at the destination in Florida,
Where no one else has been.

Sergio Mucci (10)
Stoke Park Junior School

The Magic Box
(Based on the poem 'Magic Box' by Kit Wright)

I will put in the box . . .
The spark of lightning like a golden dagger
From a storm on a threatful night,
The deepest, darkest secret from the furthest part of my mind,
Glowing in the night from cat's eyes that are like lightbulbs.

I will put in the box . . .
Laughter from a small child not knowing what's going on,
White waves washing from the sea on a windy, summer's day,
Sensitivity of a small pet that's been neglected.

I will put in the box . . .
Silver foil off a sparkling chocolate bar,
A doubtful dream of a small child on a restless night,
Waving hands and branches of a tree in the wind of a stormy night.

I will put in the box . . .
The darkness at the bottom of the ocean in a crashing storm,
Sadness of a neglected toy left alone for years,
Unhappiness of people when evil creeps over the world.

My box is fashioned from sadness and darkness,
With evil swirling all over the lid,
Its hinges are made from a child's tears.

I shall hide in my box,
In the darkest spot the eye can see,
Then stay hidden forever in the dark.

Courtney Richmond (11)
Stoke Park Junior School

The Magic Box
(Based on the poem 'Magic Box' by Kit Wright)

I will put in the box . . .
The storm of our love, hide it away forever,
Lightning, the shock when you told me,
That secret, the one you never mentioned.

I will put in the box . . .
Your beauty and the angel that you are,
The long lasting laughter of a summer's night,
That genie that I love for what he gave me.

I will put in the box . . .
The memory of that time when I was happy,
A dream, the one that is unreal,
Our love to remind me of you forever.

My box is fashioned from . . .
All my love and memories,
With secrets in the corners,
And sorrow on the lid,
Its hinges are made from my most precious dream,
The one that no one knows.

I shall hide my box,
Where no one will look,
In the one place that is truly mine,
In the deepest place in my heart,
Where it will drift around forever,
Safe and true.

Jack Howson (10)
Stoke Park Junior School

The Magic Box
(Based on the poem 'Magic Box' by Kit Wright)

I will put in the box . . .
The bark of a happy dog chasing away birds,
The darkest, hidden secrets from the depths of my mind,
A joyful memory from a summer adventure.

I will put in the box . . .
The happiness a child feels as she grows a year older,
Laughter from a giggling baby as he plays with his toys,
The warm summer breeze that is the breath of the sun.

I will put in the box . . .
A spark of lightning like a silver sword,
Sharp and pointed,
A waft of smelly blue cheese,
Like Dad's old trainers,
And smiles of a summer photo,
Hanging on the wall.

My box is fashioned from wind and rain,
With raindrops crying from the clouds in the corners,
Its hinges are the heavens.

I shall swim in my box,
On the great waves of the ocean,
Riding on dolphins, then resting on the beach.

Amelia Humphries (11)
Stoke Park Junior School

The Magic Box
(Based on the poem 'Magic Box' by Kit Wright)

I will put in my box . . .
The cry of the last laughing witch,
The first drop of the coldest river,
The first thought of a newborn baby,
Looking at its mother.

I will put in my box . . .
A shake of an earthquake from a waking mountain in Hawaii,
Laughter from the loveliest dog playing fetch,
A spark like an electric fish in water.

I will put in my box . . .
The purest blood of a pet wolf,
A grain from a white beach in Australia,
And the 10th bullet from the first gun.

My box is fashioned from dreams in the middle of the night,
With stars formed from a storm,
In the corners, souls trapped in an endless pit
Sealed by the steel from the bluest star.

I shall fight in my box on the fields of war,
Then die in agony while standing my ground,
Defending my box.

Callum Holmes (10)
Stoke Park Junior School

The Magic Box
(Based on the poem 'Magic Box' by Kit Wright)

I will put in the box . . .
The highest bounce of a kangaroo,
The sweetest taste of milky cocoa,
The spin of a carousel like a washing machine.

I will put in the box . . .
The colours of nature from trees and shrubs,
Venom in the spit of a deadly snake,
The ink of the oldest, broken pen.

I will put in the box . . .
The softest feather from the biggest pillow,
The worst storm from the jungle's air,
The shortest page of the largest book.

My box is fashioned from rings of Saturn,
With stars from corner to corner and sun on my lid,
The hinges are the flames from Mars.

I shall ride on my box,
Like a cowboy in USA,
Then park it next to the stables.

Joe Perrett (10)
Stoke Park Junior School

The Door
(Inspired by the poem 'The Door' by Miroslav Holub)

Go and open the door,
Maybe outside there's a New World,
Or a curious black, cushioned seat,
Waiting to take you to Brand Land,
A sight to see, not just any sight, a sight of the world's end,
Or a pitch-black tunnel on its way through an erupting volcano.

Go and open the door,
Maybe an approachable brown bear sits gorging
On a sparkling silver fish,
Maybe you'll see the centre of my mind,
Or a travelling TARDIS on its epic journey,
Swooping through space,
Or the gaping jaws of a mighty, golden dragon.

Go and open the door,
If there's a guard he will let you through.

Go and open the door,
Even if there's only a cardboard box,
Even if there's only a red brick wall,
Even if nothing's there,
Go and open the door . . .

James Brand (9)
Wellow Primary School

The Door
(Inspired by the poem 'The Door' by Miroslav Holub)

Go open the door,
Maybe outside there's a dragon gorging itself on a deer,
Or a sunset streaming through it,
Or a cane ready to strike.

Go and open the door,
Maybe it's just pitch-blackness,
Maybe you'll feel a wind that rattles your bones,
Or the eye of an exterminator that you will never forget.

Go and open the door,
If there's a building about to collapse onto you,
You will survive.

Go and open the door,
Even if there's stillness,
Even if there's just wind,
Even if there's nothing there,
Go and open the door.

Ross Weeks (10)
Wellow Primary School

The Door
(Inspired by the poem 'The Door' by Miroslav Holub)

Go and open the door,
Maybe there's the sad thoughts in your head to vanquish,
Or maybe your future in your next life to decide,
Or even the key to your love life crumpled, tossed and torn.

Go and open the door,
Maybe the Prime Minister will shake your hand,
Maybe you'll see the land of unknown,
Or even another door will lead you to the land of open doors,
Or maybe the witch of the west will do battle.

Go and open the door,
If there's a war you are sure to triumph.

Go and open the door,
Even if there's only a pile of ash,
Even if nothing is there,
Even if there's only a strand of hair,
Go and open the door.

Dev Daas (9)
Wellow Primary School

The Door
(Inspired by the poem 'The Door' by Miroslav Holub)

Go and open the door . . .
Maybe outside is the key to your future,
Or a riddle ready to be solved,
Or pictures of happiness and childhood,
A day with no name . . .

Go and open the door . . .
Maybe you will be on top of the metallic moon,
Maybe there is a ship sailing forever searching for jubilation,
Or a never, ever, ending fairytale . . .

Go and open the door . . .
If there's a fire,
It will expire . . .

Go and open the door . . .
Even if there is a broken black hole,
Even if nothing is there . . .

Go and open the door!

Cara Young (9)
Wellow Primary School

The Door
(Inspired by the poem 'The Door' by Miroslav Holub)

Go and open the door . . .
Maybe outside there's a cave,
Maybe it will wave and say, 'Welcome,'
Or a field of doubt gently swaying in the breeze of hope,
Or a room, the room of mystery.

Go and open the door . . .
Maybe a box will glow with a hundred fantasies,
Maybe you will see the Goddess of Chaos,
Or maybe there's a dragon of happiness waiting to pounce,
Or a rock who will stand tall and proud in the water,
And open the door . . .
If there's a mist, it will be warm and pass quickly.

Go and open the door . . .
Even if there's none of this there,
Even if there is nothing there at all,
Even if there is no opportunity for you,
Go and open the door.

Laura Overton-Hore (10)
Wellow Primary School

The Door
(Inspired by the poem 'The Door' by Miroslav Holub)

Go and open the door,
Maybe outside there's
A ruby red dragon,
Or the door to your thoughts,
Or the key to your past,
Or a parallel universe at war.

Go and open the door,
Maybe there's a bongo escaping poachers, hunting for skin,
Maybe you'll see the heart of the world, beating,
Or a golden lion stalking his prey,
Or a guru waiting to teach you the way of the Jedi.

Go and open the door,
If you come across a marsh,
Walk over it.

Go and open the door,
Maybe there's a drop of gum on a golden doorstep,
Or an open door in a door,
Or chocolate apples for the future,
Or a time lord from the past,
Even if there's nothing there,
Go and open the door.

Kyran Hansford (11)
Wellow Primary School

The Door
(Inspired by the poem 'The Door' by Miroslav Holub)

Go and open the door,
Outside there may be . . .
An open-mouthed marsh waiting to swallow you,
Or a magic carpet to whisk you away,
Or a bed of petals for you and your love.

Go and open the door,
Maybe a key to the past hovers,
Maybe you'll see a wide ocean winking in the sun,
Or your dream car to drive to the end of time,
Or you'll witness an unforgiving earthquake.

Go and open the door,
If there's a darkness . . .
A light of love will shine.

Go and open the door,
Even if there's the end of the world,
Go and open the door,
Even if there's only the empty silence,
Go and open the door.

Even if there's nothing there,
Go and open . . . the door!

Annabel Skinner (9)
Wellow Primary School

The Door
(Inspired by the poem 'The Door' by Miroslav Holub)

Go and open the door,
Maybe outside there's a jungle to explore,
A whale,
A lion,
Or even the last sight of another door.

Go and open the door,
Maybe you'll see an alligator's jaw,
Maybe you'll find a dinosaur,
Or even a fictional, leopard skin store.

Go and open the door,
If there's an element you will find the secrets of the law.

Go and open the door,
Find a dragon guarding its precious egg,
Even if there's a mighty phoenix bowing his head.

Go and open the door,
Even if there's nothing there,
Go and open the door.

Kyle Russell Blakey (11)
Wellow Primary School

The Door
(Inspired by the poem 'The Door' by Miroslav Holub)

Go and open the door,
Maybe outside there's a golden, glistening sunset,
Or a killer whale savage and brave,
Or a historic fossil from the beginning of time.

Go and open the door,
Maybe you'll see a fantastic flock of fish,
Maybe you'll see the desert plains,
Or the poles from a million miles above.

Go and open the door,
If there's a inconceivable monster,
It shall wither and die.

Go and open the door,
Even if there's only a little spark,
Even if there's only a rose without its thorns,
Even if there's only a tree without its crisp, green leaves,
Even if there's nothing there, go and open the door.

Harry Chapman (10)
Wellow Primary School

The Door
(Inspired by the poem 'The Door' by Miroslav Holub)

Go and open the door,
Maybe outside there's,
A magic ball showing you your future which is waiting for you,
Or a flying dragon begging for you to climb on its back.

Go and open the door,
Maybe a box sits there full of your wishes,
Maybe you'll see a mirror that can transport you to your dreams,
Or maybe a magical island, with a golden treasure chest,
Or a special spider's web that catches your horrible thoughts.

Go and open the door,
If there's a flashing storm,
It will lessen.

Go and open the door,
Even if there's a mud splattered parcel,
Even if there's a cloud grey path,
Even if nothing is there,
Go and open the door.

Lauren Williams (10)
Wellow Primary School

The Door
(Inspired by the poem 'The Door' by Miroslav Holub)

Go and open the door,
Maybe outside there's a dove of love that will grant you a wish or two,
Maybe outside there's a land of your unseen relatives,
Waiting to be discovered,
Or a baking beach with sunbathing waves.

Go and open the door,
Maybe there's a key to unlock your inner self,
Maybe you'll see a land of fun and laughter,
Or the secret to save all endangered animals,
Or a future of glowing joy with a happy ever after.

Go and open the door,
If there's a wall, it will vanish,
Go and open the door,
Even if there's a beggar you cannot help,
Even if there's just a speck of dust,
Even if there's nothing there, go and open the door.

Rhiannon Lloyd Leighton (9)
Wellow Primary School

The Door
(Inspired by the poem 'The Door' by Miroslav Holub)

Go and open the door,
Maybe outside there are sunbeams glistening down
On snow-capped mountains,
Or maybe an underwater world where fish glide past your
Face like lollipops,
Or a key to your friendship kept together with glue
Or tossed away into the dustbin.

Go and open the door,
Maybe there's a tree of your winged wishes whizzing around,
Maybe you'll see your future beyond you,
Or your imagination bubbling with fantasies,
Or a magical garden with pixies daintily dancing
Around a withered oak.

Go and open the door,
If there's a tornado, it will pass as quick as lightning.

Go and open the door,
Even if only the deep sea sleeps,
Even if there's only the twirling mist around you,
Even if nothing is there,
Go and open the door.

Grace Oreffo (10)
Wellow Primary School

The Door
(Inspired by the poem 'The Door' by Miroslav Holub)

Go and open the door,
Maybe outside there's a perfect world from your dreams,
A land of glory could be there,
Or a chance to have the life desired by many people.

Go and open the door,
Maybe a world of only chocolate is there for the eating,
Maybe you'll see a door leading to the door of life and death,
Or the dead spirits could be floating high above you,
Searching for life,
Or the end of planet Earth could be in front of your eyes.

Go and open the door,
If there's a pig-like alien,
Then be calm and it will spare you.

Go and open the door,
Even if there's only disasters and dread,
Even if there's only darkness and gloom,
Even if nothing is there,
Go and open the door.

Adam Cater (10)
Wellow Primary School

The Door
(Inspired by the poem 'The Door' by Miroslav Holub)

Go and open the door,
Maybe outside there's a thunderous wall of sharp, frozen snow,
An antique locket full of burning nightmares,
Or a magical world to all of your dreams.

Go and open the door,
Maybe a ghostly spirit has appeared to take over your soul,
Maybe you'll observe your future life as an adult,
Or another eccentric door might be waiting for you,
Or a secret map of a mysterious house might lie there.

Go and open the door,
If there's a wall high wave, it will lower.

Go and open the door,
Even if there's only an ancient, dusty novel,
Even if there's only some ordinary lilies,
Even if nothing is there,
Go and open the door!

Monica Young (9)
Wellow Primary School

The Door
(Inspired by the poem 'The Door' by Miroslav Holub)

Go and open the door,
There could be an assault on Earth,
Or a great, mythical legend,
Or possibly Jesus' birth.

Go and open the door,
Maybe you'll see a football Cup Final,
Or you could see a stegosaurus crying for help,
You might see a sandy shore on a lost island.

Go and open the door,
If there's a drooling spider, it will perish.

Go and open the door,
Even if there's only room for one,
Even if there's only a shattered heart,
Even if nothing is there,
Go and open the door.

Edward Barnes (10)
Wellow Primary School

The Door
(Inspired by the poem 'The Door' by Miroslav Holub)

Go and open the door,
Maybe outside there's the end of a world never known,
Never forgotten,
Or a tiger waiting to pounce,
Or a killer bee's sting,
Or a carnivorous dinosaur's bite.

Go and open the door,
Maybe outside there's
A Hiponostriphicow,
Or a door to a door to a door to a door . . .
Or a killer alien,
Or a homeless bird.

Go and open the door,
If there's a plague,
You will vanquish it.

Go and open the door,
Even if there's a fading life,
Even if there's only a broken heart,
Even if there's nothing at all there,
Go and open the door.

Dan Cullen (9)
Wellow Primary School

The Door
(Inspired by the poem 'The Door' by Miroslav Holub)

Go and open the door,
Maybe outside there is a midnight cat strolling the streets,
For discarded fish bones,
Or a room full of people you've always loved,
Or a book full of everybody's secrets and wishes.

Go and open the door,
Maybe outside there is a trunk full to the brim
With treasure and jewels,
Maybe you'll see two fangs from a king cobra
That still have a drop of poison on them,
Or a swan's feather that has been used for a quill
By a wise wizard.

Go and open the door,
Even if there is a rose red ruby that is the key to the future,
Even if there's a fairytale chest full of happiness and love,
Go and open the door,
Even if there's only a nightingale singing sweet lullabies,
Even if there's only a door to your imagination,
Even if you open the door to find nothing is there,
Open the door.

Eleanor Sandison (10)
Wellow Primary School

The Door
(Inspired by the poem 'The Door' by Miroslav Holub)

Go and open the door,
Maybe outside there's an emerald cave,
Or a treasure chest of destiny,
Maybe there's the key to friendship and love,
Or a magical land pulling you in.

Go and open the door,
Maybe outside all your dreams come true,
Or a hand to greet you,
Or a lifetime of chocolate,
Or your favourite football team lifting the World Cup.

Go and open the door,
If there are evil forces, then they will perish.

Go and open the door,
Even if there's only your family with loving comments,
Even if there's nothing there,
Go and open the door.

Oliver Lambert (9)
Wellow Primary School

The Door
(Inspired by the poem 'The Door' by Miroslav Holub)

Go on and open the door,
Maybe outside there's a path
That leads you to destructive darkness,
Or a path to a hero's greatness,
Or the end of the world.

Go and open the door,
Maybe the key of life will be free to heal the world from death,
Maybe you'll see a tower full of secrets,
Or a magical zoo full of masterful animals,
Or a portal to a different dimension.

Go on and open the door,
Even if there are only a couple of weak clouds
Floating in the air,
Even if there's only a dull school lesson,
Even if there's nothing there,
Go and open the door.

Jackson Howell (9)
Wellow Primary School

The Door
(Inspired by the poem 'The Door' by Miroslav Holub)

Go and open the door . . .

Maybe outside there's a Roman god,
Watching his people roam his creation,
Or maybe you feel your life dissolving into nothingness,
Or maybe you witness your last words and
Your last laugh before being carried to your grave.

Go and open the door . . .

Maybe you'll see the last surviving planet,
All crippled and torn, swallowed by a black hole,
Maybe you'll see the first human to ever walk the Earth,
Or maybe you'll survey a star burning its last rays,
Maybe you open the door to your dreams.

Go and open the door . . .

If you are caught in a storm,
You will brave through.

Go and open the door . . .

Even if you sense yourself as a spirit floating in Heaven,
Even if climate change is at its pinnacle,
Destroying everything in its path,
Even if there's nothing,
Go and open the door . . .

Simon Lockyer (10)
Wellow Primary School

The Door
(Inspired by the poem 'The Door' by Miroslav Holub)

Go and open the door,
Maybe outside there is a clown with a green nose,
Or maybe there is a Caribbean beach
Ready for a holiday,
Or a wolf ready to pounce,
Maybe there is a poor, abandoned,
Dog in the streets,
Or a suspicious murderer.

Go and open the door,
Maybe there is the key to life,
Or a pair of cheeky monkeys swinging
From the trees in a Brazilian rainforest,
There might be an alien on a bike like ET.

Go and open the door,
Even if there are clouds and grey sky, it will not rain.

Go and open the door,
There might be a world of happiness.

Go and open the door,
There might be a moon from another world,
Or a wary, maybe it is World War III.

Go and open the door,
Even if there is only just the bare wind there for the taking,
If there is only a twig, twenty years old.

Go and open the door,
Even if there is nothing there.

Go and open the door . . .

Daniel Williams (10)
Wellow Primary School

Young Writers Information

We hope you have enjoyed reading this book - and that you will continue to enjoy it in the coming years.

If you like reading and writing poetry drop us a line, or give us a call, and we'll send you a free information pack.

Alternatively if you would like to order further copies of this book or any of our other titles, then please give us a call or log onto our website at
www.youngwriters.co.uk

Young Writers Information
Remus House
Coltsfoot Drive
Peterborough
PE2 9JX

(01733) 890066